The Wit
of the Jews

The Wit
of the Jews

Compiled by

Lore and Maurice Cowan

Aurora Publishers Incorporated
NASHVILLE/LONDON

FIRST PUBLISHED 1970
LESLIE FREWIN PUBLISHERS LIMITED
LONDON, ENGLAND

COPYRIGHT © 1970 BY
AURORA PUBLISHERS INCORPORATED
NASHVILLE, TENNESSEE 37219
LIBRARY OF CONGRESS CATALOG CARD NUMBER: 75-129524
STANDARD BOOK NUMBER: 87695-114-0
MANUFACTURED IN THE UNITED STATES OF AMERICA

CONTENTS

Introduction

KNOWING THE IMPOSSIBILITY of putting hundreds of gallons into a pint pot, it would be imprudent of us – even impertinent – not to point out to our readers that this volume is but a 'sample' of the wit of the Jews.

This wit is a chronicle of a people's experience over thousands of years and, as such, has astounded and bewildered the world; the Jewish experience remains one of the greatest enigmas. The wit of the Jew was often a commentary on his treatment by a cruel world that refused to allow him to put down roots for any length of time. When roots were sunk, it was in a ghetto, yet no ghetto could keep the Jew from laughing, or from exercising his wit, the only weapon that he had.

He has laughed at the world, and at himself, even in the most tragic situations. The more the Jew suffered, the more he protested with his wit against his persecutors, but, so often, beneath the smile there was a tear.

The Jew believes in the old Jewish saying – 'Does your heart ache? – Laugh it off.' The assertion of the Polish scientist, Alexander Moskowski (1851–1934), that 'Jewish wit is the foundation and pinnacle of all wit' may be too sweeping, yet who but a Jew would converse privately with God, and say – 'Thou hast chosen us from among all nations – what, O Lord, did you have against us?'

We wish to emphasise that the word 'Jew' is not used in its religious sense. The term is used in its broadest sense to include such people as Disraeli, Heine, Spinoza, who were born Jews of Jewish parents, even though they later adopted another faith.

LC
MC

From the Four Corners of the Earth

Bible students are still debating whether the teasing by Elijah (circa 860 BC) of the Priests of Baal (Kings 1, ch. 18), was the first recorded wit of a Jew, or whether it was purely irony.

Some scholars assert that there is considerable wit in the books of Proverbs and Ecclesiastes, incorrectly attributed to King Solomon (917–931 BC). But all agree with the witticism of an unknown Alexandrian Jew, who, recalling the sad fate of Lot's wife, wrote in the Apocrypha, about 100 BC:

A disbelieving soul has a memorial. a pillar of salt.

Alfred Adler (1870–1937)
Austrian psychologist

It is easier to fight for principles than to live up to them.

*　　　*　　　*

Samuel Joseph Agnon
Israeli Nobel-prize novelist

No midgets, no giants.

The end of all learning is forgetting.

*   *   *

Ahad Ha Am (1856-1927)
Russian essayist

('One of the People', pen name of Asher Ginzberg.)

I am very careful in the choice of enemies.

In 1915

The man I envy more than anybody else is Shackleton, who managed to get away in time to the South Pole – the only place to which the stench of 'humanity' certainly cannot reach.

*   *   *

Solomon Ansky (S J Rappaport) (1863-1920)
Russian-Yiddish writer, author of the famous play 'The Dybbuk'

A worm can enter a fruit only after it has begun to rot.

A rich miser called on a rabbi. The good man led him to the window and asked him what he saw.
'People,' answered the miser.
The rabbi then led him to a mirror.
'What do you see now?'

'I see myself.'
Said the rabbi:

There is glass in the window and there is glass in the mirror, but in the mirror the glass is covered with a little silver, and no sooner is a little silver added than you cease to regard others and see only yourself.

*   *   *

Sholem Asch (1881-1957)
Yiddish novelist and playwright

On writing

It is much like writing a cheque: it is easy to write one if you have enough money in the bank, and writing comes more easily if you have something to say.

The best security for old age – respect your children.

When a downward-thrusting root encounters a stone and cannot split it, it seeks ways of getting round it.

*   *   *

Gregory Bar-Hebraeus (1226-1286)
Syrian physician and philosopher

As long as a word remaineth unspoken it is in the prison

of him that wished to speak, but when once it hath been spoken the speaker thereof becometh its prisoner.

A rich man, who was a clown, never gave anything to a poor man. He used to say, 'That which God hath not given him, how can I give him?'

*   *   *

Vicki Baum (1888-1961)
Austrian-American novelist

To be a Jew is a destiny.

Marriage always demands the greatest understanding of the art of insincerity possible between two human beings.

Pity is the deadliest feeling that can be offered to a woman.

You don't get ulcers from what you eat. You get them from what's eating you.

To me writing is not a profession. You might as well call living a profession. Or having children. Anything you can't help doing.

Once you're publicly stamped as having lost that literary virginity because some of your books happened to become best sellers, you'll never be able to clear your name.

You can live down any amount of failures; but you can't live down a great success.

When we are young our parents run our life; when we get older, our children do.

Success is as ice cold and lonely as the North Pole.

A woman who is loved always has success.

*   *   *

S N Behrman
Eminent American dramatist and biographer

My ambition is to be a critic-at-large of things – as – they – are. I want to reduce the whole system to absurdity. I want to laugh the powers-that-be out of existence in great winnowing gales of laughter.

Most autobiographies are written by corpses.

I think immortality is an overrated commodity.

Foreigners are people, you know. Some of them are rather nice.

On Lord Duveen, the art dealer:

Probably never before had a merchant brought to such

B

exquisite perfection the large-mindest art of casting bread upon the waters.

In all love affairs there comes a moment when desire demands possession.

*The philosophy of a Jewish Polish refugee, Jacobowsky, the principal character in the film **Me and the Colonel** written by S. N. Behrman and George Froeschel, based on the play by Franz Werfel.*

I don't know anything about miracles, but my mother, wise woman that she was, used to say that no matter what happens in life there are always two possibilities. For instance, even in this dark moment there are two possibilities. Either the Germans will come to Paris, or they'll turn to the English Channel. If they don't come to Paris, that's good. But if they *should* come to Paris, there are two possibilities. Either they spare the city or they bomb it. If they spare the city, that's good; but if they bomb it, there are two possibilities. Either you escape or you're buried in the rubble. If you escape, that's good, but if you're buried in the rubble . . .

From the biography by S N Behrman on:

Lord Duveen (1869–1939)
The greatest art dealer in history

On pictures:

An accumulation is never a collection.

To an American industrialist, who had no pictures, and wanted to buy a Rembrandt:

I can't possibly sell a Rembrandt to a man who owns no other pictures. The Rembrandt would be lonely.

To an American lady who protested that a Renaissance portrait of a girl had been restored:

My dear Madam, if you were as old as this young girl, you would have to be restored too.

*   *   *

David Ben-Gurion
Former Prime Minister of Israel

In Israel, in order to be a realist, you must believe in miracles.

On a visit to California:

I envy your deserts – not just because they are deserts, but because you can afford to keep them deserts.

The outlook of the ghetto divided the Universe into two: this world for the Gentiles, the hereafter for the Jews.

There is one thing a man cannot change – his parents.

Thinking is a strenuous art – few practise it; and then only at rare times.

On television in Israel:

A nation surrounded by Arabs has no need of cowboys and Indians.

*   *   *

Judah P Benjamin (1811-1884)
American statesman and lawyer

On his fees as a lawyer:

First I charge a retainer, then I charge a reminder, next I charge a refresher, and then I charge a finisher.

*   *   *

Bernard Berenson (1865-1959)
World famous art expert and critic

My house is a library with living-rooms attached.

Like the ants, the Jews never lose faith in life – Hamans and Hitlers everywhere; yet they live on and enjoy life.

Jews are scapegoats for economic sins.

Governments last as long as the undertaxed can defend them against the overtaxed.

*   *   *

Henri Bergson (1859-1941)
French philosopher

Sex-appeal is the keynote of our whole civilisation.

Homo Sapiens: the only creature endowed with reason, is also the only creature to pin its existence to things unreasonable.

*   *   *

Leonard Bernstein
American composer and conductor

Comment on a popular stage musical:

I walked out infuriated after the first act. The lyrics are just laundry lists.

*   *   *

Lord Bernstein
Head of Granada TV, theatres and publishing companies

Asked why he chose the North as his operational area for Granada TV:

17

I looked at two maps. One showed population density. The other showed rainfall.

Commenting on his father's ownership of cinemas:

I was born with a silver screen in my mouth.

*   *   *

Léon Blum (1872–1949)
One-time French Premier

In critical times men can save their lives only by risking them.

*   *   *

Ludwig Boerne (1786–1837)
German writer

The world is a mirror. It returns what you lend it.

We must bow reverently before children. They are our masters; we work for them.

A woman lives only when she loves. She finds herself only when she loves herself in a man.

The distance between one and nothing is greater than between one and a thousand.

Shrewdness is often annoying, like a lamp in a bedroom.

Pain is the father, and love the mother of wisdom.

Understanding is bread which satisfies. Wit is the spice that makes it appetising.

From Heaven we get comfort, but from people we expect assistance.

There are many things men can do without, men excepted.

A diplomat has to learn three things: to speak French, to say nothing, and to tell lies.

The difference between liberty and liberties is as great as between God and gods.

The Holy Roman Empire – neither holy, nor Roman, nor an empire.

That two diplomats can look at each other without laughing amazes me.

Riches harden the heart faster than boiling water does an egg.

To regret nothing is the beginning of all wisdom.

An hour spent in hate is an eternity withdrawn from love.

Humour is a gift of the heart, not of the mind.

Ministers fall like buttered bread, usually on the good side.

Peoples are liberated through impatience, not through patience.

Jealousy makes a man silly, but a woman more subtle.

A sweetheart is milk, a bride is butter, and a wife is cheese.

Man is like a musical clock – move him even slightly and he begins to sing a new tune.

*   *   *

Art Buchwald
American journalist and essayist

Old soldiers never die – they just write their memoirs.

Art Buchwald's Paris:

Any fair-minded observer, comparing the behaviour of the average dog with that of the average customer in a Paris restaurant, would side with the dog every time.
I have never seen a dog acting pedantic over a wine list.
I have never seen a dog send back an exquisite steak with the demand that the chef overcook it.

Any sportsman will tell you that the only three things to see in the Louvre are the 'Winged Victory of Samothrace', the 'Venus de Milo', and the 'Mona Lisa'.

The rest of the sculpture and paintings are just so much window dressing for the Big Three. Ever since the Louvre acquired these works of art, amateurs all over the world have been trying to cut down the time it takes to see them. In 1949 a track star from Miami University made it in six minutes and fourteen seconds. In 1951 the Australians took the title away from the Americans with a six-minute-twelve-second Louvre.

By this time everyone was talking about a six-minute Louvre. Scientists said that under perfect conditions, with a smooth floor, excellent lighting, and no wind, it could be done.

After an American had beaten the record with five minutes fifty-six seconds he said –

'The next record I'm going after is St Peter's in Rome, and then, who knows, perhaps I'll try the Tower of London. They say you can't do it in less than four minutes. Well, let's just see.'

It is obvious that with all the heads of state visiting each other we're entering into an era of gastronomic diplomacy. Instead of the world ending with a whimper or a bang, it could easily end with a burp. It is expected that a Gastronomic Disarmament Conference will be called at Maxims. One of the reasons the United States won't agree on total Gastro-Disarmament is that the Russians will probably refuse to allow the West to inspect the kitchens. Anyone who has ever eaten in a Moscow restaurant will know why.

*   *   *

Al Capp
American cartoonist and columnist

Anybody who gets out of college having had his confidence in the perfection of existing institutions affirmed has not been educated. Just suffocated.

The public is like a piano. You just have to know what keys to poke.

All I do is to suggest that nothing is perfect. This gets some people perfectly furious at me, and they complain they're being attacked.

Those parents who concern themselves with their children's problems are crazy. The problems of a nine-year-old kid cannot be solved in any way, except by becoming ten.

Don't be a pal to your son. Be his father. What child needs a 40-year-old man for a friend.

*   *   *

Hermann Cohen (1842-1918)
German philosopher

An anti-semite may prove 'logically' that Jesus never existed, and may yet prove 'historically' that the Jews had crucified him.

*   *   *

Shalom Cohen (1772-1845)
Polish author

No rain, no fruit, no toil, no good.

A brilliant mind without faith is like a beautiful face without eyes.

*   *   *

Art Cohn (d 1958)
American author

During the depression in America in 1931:

No four-letter word was as obscene as *bank*. It was short for bankrupt.

Of Mike Todd, whose biography he wrote:

He was born with an inability to look backward.

On Hollywood:

A village of tasteless producers and scentless flowers, controlled by frightened little men armed with buckets of sand to extinguish any fires of creative originality that might break out.

Love has no foundation in reason, therefore it cannot be thought out or talked out. It has to wear out.

*   *   *

Aaron Copland
Dean of American composers

Music has become so very accessible, it is almost impossible to avoid it.

*   *   *

Benjamin Disraeli (1804-1881)
Famous Prime Minister of England

In answer to the Irish MP Daniel O'Connell, who made fun of Disraeli's Jewish ancestry:

Yes, I am a Jew, and when the ancestors of the right honourable gentleman were brutal savages in an unknown island, mine were priests in the Temple of Solomon.

To govern men, you must either excel them in their accomplishments or despise them.

I may commit many follies in my life, but I never intend to marry for 'love', which I am sure is a guarantee for infelicity.

You must not contrast too strongly the hours of courtship with the years of possession.

I never trouble to be avenged. When a man injures me I put his name on a piece of paper and lock it up in a drawer. It is marvellous to see how the men I have thus labelled have the knack of disappearing.

Definition of a lawyer:

Ever illustrating the obvious, explaining the evident – and expatiating the commonplace.

A want of tact is worse than a want of virtue.

Every man has the right to be conceited until he is successful.

No one is pelted so much as a political apostate, except, perhaps a religious one.

On Sir Robert Peel:

A burglar of other's intellect – there is no statesman who has committed political larceny on so grand a scale.

The right honourable gentleman is reminiscent of a poker. The only difference is that a poker gives off occasional signs of warmth.

The right honourable gentleman's smile is like the silver fittings on a coffin.

Everyone likes flattery, and when you come to Royalty, you should lay it on with a trowel.

His recipe for pleasing Queen Victoria:

I never deny, I never contradict; I sometimes forget.

On being told that John Bright was a self-made man:

I know he is, and he adores his maker.

To a suggestion that Disraeli might use in an election an illicit love affair of Palmerston, Disraeli replied:

Palmerston is now seventy. If he could provide evidence of his potency in his electoral address, he'd sweep the country.

Life is too short to be little.

If every man were straightforward in his opinions, there would be no conversation. The fun of talk is to find what a man really thinks, and then contrast it with the enormous lies he has been telling all dinner, and perhaps all his life.

His reply to Dean Stanley who suggested that the Athanasian Creed should be deleted from the Book of Common Prayer:

Mr Dean, no dogmas, no deans.

I have always thought that every woman should marry and no man.

No man is regular in his attendance in the House of Commons until he is married.

You should treat a cigar like a mistress; put it away before you are sick of it.

When heckled at a meeting by the shout of 'Speak up! I can't ear you,' he retorted:

Truth travels slowly, but it will reach even you in time.

I have often observed that nothing ever perplexes an adversary so much as an appeal to his honour.

Nobody is forgotten when it is convenient to remember him.

You know who the critics are? The men who have failed in literature and art.

An author who speaks about his own books is almost as bad as a mother who talks about her own children.

When asked about the difference between a misfortune and a alamity:

Well, if Gladstone fell into the Thames, that would be a misfortune; and if anybody pulled him out, that, I suppose, would be a calamity.

When I meet a man whose name I can't remember, I give

myself two minutes, and then if it is a hopeless case, I always say, 'And how is the old complaint?'

How much easier to be critical than to be correct.

During his illness the nurse wanted to put an air-cushion behind his back:

No, no, take away that emblem of mortality.

As he was dying, correcting the proofs of his last speech:

I will not go down to posterity talking bad grammar.

*   *   *

Isaac d'Israeli (1766-1848)
Writer, father of Benjamin Disraeli

Some will read old books, as if there were no valuable truths to be discovered in modern publications.

Great collections of books are subject to certain accidents besides the damp, the worms, and the rats; one not less common is that of the *borrowers,* not to say a word of the purloiners.

A circle may be small, yet it may be as mathematically beautiful and perfect as a large one.

The Self-Educated are marked by stubborn peculiarities.

Fortune has rarely condescended to be the companion of genius.

The calmest husbands make the stormiest wives.

The wise make proverbs and fools repeat them.

The magic of first love is our ignorance that it can ever end.

A majority is always the best repartee.

*　　　*　　　*

Abba Eban
Israeli statesman

The identity of views between two governments is a sign of trouble for one of them.

*　　　*　　　*

Albert Einstein (1879-1955)
World-famous scientist

If my theory of relativity is proven successful, Germany will claim me as a German and France will declare that I am a citizen of the world. If my theory should prove to be untrue, then France will say that I am a German, and Germany will say that I am a Jew.

C

God does not play at dice.

In answer to a question he once replied:

I don't know. Why fill my memory with facts that I can find in an encyclopaedia.

Thanking Bernard Shaw for a reference to himself:

It is addressed to my mythical namesake who makes my life a singular burden.

We cannot despair of humanity since we are only human ourselves.

Tyrants of genius are succeeded by scoundrels.

Science without religion is lame; religion without science is blind.

Nationalism is an infantile disease. It is the measles of mankind.

The road to perdition has always been accompanied by lip service to an ideal.

An empty stomach is not a good political adviser.

I never think of the future. It comes soon enough.

Education is that which remains when one has forgotten everything he learned in school.

People flatter me as long as I do not embarrass them.

God is clever but he is not dishonest.

The most incomprehensible thing about the world is that it is comprehensible.

ked by his hostess at a social gathering to explain his Theory Relativity:

'Madam, I was once walking in the country on a hot day, with a blind friend and remarked that I would like a drink of milk.'
'I understand drink,' said my friend, 'but what is milk?'
'A white liquid,' I replied.
'I know liquid, but what is white?'
'The same colour as a swan's feathers.'
'I know feathers, but what is a swan?'
'A bird with a crooked neck.'
'I know neck, but what is crooked?'
I lost my patience. I seized his arm and straightened it. Then I bent it at the elbow and said, 'That is crooked.'
'Ah,' said my blind companion, 'now I know what you mean by milk.'

When Mrs Einstein visited the Mt Wilson Observatory in California she admired the giant telescope and its attachments, and asked what they were for.

They told her that one of the chief uses was to find out th
shape of the Universe.
'Oh,' replied Mrs Einstein, 'my husband does that on th
back of an old envelope!'

My life is a simple thing that would interest no one. It
a known fact that I was born and that is all that is nece
sary.

Definition of Relativity:

When a man sits for an hour with a pretty girl on h
knee, it seems like a minute. But let him sit on a h
stove for a minute – and it's longer than an hour.
That's relativity.

Defining success:

If A equals success, then the formula is A equals X pl
Y plus Z. X is work, Y is play, Z is keep your mouth sh

*   *   *

Jacob Epstein (1880-1959)
Famous sculptor

Asked if he thought that one of his figures was his greatest wor

I'm modest enough to say that they're all great.

A bohemian is a man who plays all night and sleeps all day. I have always worked too hard to be considered a bohemian.

I do my work in a storm of controversy, somewhat like the atmosphere of a boxing ring, with adherents and enemies shouting encouragement and abuse to each other.

Epstein's studio was covered with newspapers when Lord Beaverbrook entered. Instantly he said petulantly: 'I do not see my papers here.'
'Do you imagine,' replied Epstein, 'that I would have your papers to be trodden on?'

The model who just sits and leaves the artist to his own thoughts is the helpful one. It seems to me that Mona Lisa said nothing, that 'enigmatic' smile was quite enough for Leonardo to bother about.

The successful portrait sculptor needs a front of brass, the hide of a rhinoceros, and all the guile of a courtier.

There is something in the art–dealing business, an element of gambling, which can convert an ordinary business man into a potential inmate of a jail sooner than almost any other occupation.

*   *   *

Levi Eshkol (1895-1969)
One-time Prime Minister of Israel

Put three Zionists in a room, and they'll form fou
political parties.

*　　　*　　　*

Ludwig Fulda (1862-1939)
German playwright

Men occasionally find a new truth, but never an ol
button.

If time is money then everybody lives beyond his mean

*　　　*　　　*

Montagu Glass (1877-1934)
*Playwright—creator of the famous characters Potash
and Perlmutter*

On a salesman:

He couldn't sell a glass of water in the Sahara Desert.

The man that invented partners had a grudge against th
human race.

Don't send me a cheque. We'll wait for the money.

Looking up concerns you don't sell merchandise to is like smelling the cooking which other people is going to eat.

A lady who could still dance at fifty ain't got no excuse why she shouldn't have got married at twenty.

*   *   *

Louis Golding (1895-1958)
Novelist

> You have made a lovely world,
> O Lord, but not a wise one!

On Ireland:

Heaven help us, they are all poets, not only their writers, but their dock labourers, their barmaids, their ploughmen.

*   *   *

Judah Gordon (1831-1892)
Russian poet and writer

We have bat's eyes for our own faults, and eagle's eyes for the faults of others.

*   *   *

Philip Guedella (1889–1944)
Essayist and historian

Any stigma will serve to beat a dogma.

An Englishman is a man, who lives on an island in the North Sea, governed by Scotsmen.

Greatness is so often a courteous synonym for great success.

History is the study of other people's mistakes.

Success is little more than a chemical compound of men and moment.

Reticence has become one of the lost arts.

Almost all people who do anything in England have got something better to do. The tragedy is that they rarely do it.

One hates to hit a platitude when it is down.

Even our solicitor cannot understand his Income Tax return, and hates the man who sent it. Now the whole world is kin.

No landscape is ever enjoyed by those gifted persons who know the names of all the plants in it.

Economists are perpetually trying to lend interest to a dull subject by giving the most exciting names to singularly unexciting events. When eighty-five stout gentlemen with large cigars lose a great deal of money, which they had not yet made, they call it a Crisis. When two hundred and sixty-three stockbrokers make an undue noise in a large building in New York, they call it a Panic.

The War Office – that overcrowded cemetery of British reputations.

I had always imagined that Cliché was a suburb of Paris until I discovered it to be a street in Oxford.

No one, it would seem, has fairly estimated the indebtedness of architecture to lunatics. Most palaces and several towns owe their present form to the dementia of royal persons.

The sons of great men are, for most of us, the boys that never grow up.

On politics:

The taste for parents, which turns in foreigners to idle sentiment, is put by the British system to practical use. If a man has a father one may rely on him. If he has a grandfather, one may return him unopposed. If he has two, an early Under-Secretaryship is assured.

Last lines of his book 'Ignes Fatui':

> Here is a Book; and there's little I like of it,
> Much a Blue Pencil could easily strike of it,
> More that a cleverer Hand could amend of it;
> What does it matter? For here is an End of it.

*   *   *

Mark Hambourg (1879-1960)
Notable concert pianist

Intelligence is not needed for luck, but luck is needed for intelligence.

Money is a wonderful thing, but it's possible to pay too high a price for it.

*   *   *

Jascha Heifetz
American virtuoso violinist

You always hear of the delicate, sensitive artist. I assure you that it takes the nerve of a bull-fighter, the digestion of a peasant, the vitality of a night-club hostess, the tact of a diplomat, and the concentration of a Tibetan monk, to lead the life of a virtuoso.

Man is trying to make something for himself rather than something of himself.

*   *   *

Heinrich Heine (1797-1856)

German poet and considered by many critics to be the wittiest Jew who has ever lived

The aristocracy is composed chiefly of asses – asses who talk about horses.

Of a minor poet:

All women love him – all except the muses.

Honeymoons pass so quickly.

What falsehood lies in kisses.

In love, as in the Roman Catholic religion, there is a provisional purgatory in which one gets used to being roasted before one goes to the real, eternal hell.

If anyone asks you how I am, tell him 'like a fish in water', or rather, tell people that when one fish in the sea asks another how he is, he will get the reply: 'I am like Heine in Paris.'

> If thy tongue offend thee tear it out.
> If thine eye offend thee pluck it out.
> If thy hand offend thee cut it off.
> And if thy brain offend thee, turn Catholic.

Are the noses of the Jews so long because Jehovah has led them by the nose for 2000 years? Or are their noses a sort of uniform by which the god-King Jehovah can pick out the members of his bodyguard even when they have deserted?

The grandeur of the world is always in accordance with the grandeur of the mind that contemplates it. The good finds his paradise here, the bad already his hell.

When the arrow leaves the bow it no longer belongs to the archer, and when the word leaves the lips it is no longer controlled by the speaker.

Our German summers are but winters painted green.

Are not apes all good comedians?

The fundamental evil of the world arose from the fact that the good Lord had not created enough money.

Who never acted foolishly was also never wise.

Great misery may lodge in a little bosom.

All women are as frail as any porcelain.

Gunpowder makes men equal. A citizen's musket fires as well as a nobleman's.

If a Prince wears a Bohemian glass stone on his finger, it will be taken for a diamond; if a beggar should wear a genuine diamond ring, everyone will be convinced that it is only glass.

Virtue will last when beauty has passed.

No man can give comfort, only Time. Time heals all our wounds, only to deal our hearts fresh ones with his scythe.

I went to see Rothschild, and saw a gold-laced lackey bringing the baronial chamber pot along the corridor. A speculator from the bourse, who was passing, reverently lifted his hat to the impressive vessel. I have committed the name of the man to memory. I am quite sure that he will become a millionaire in time.

Wise men think out their thoughts; fools proclaim them.

What poetry there is in human tears!

Here's to matrimony, the high seas for which no compass has yet been invented.

Stars in which one no longer believes grow pale.

We can seldom see a flaw in a bell. We must hear its ring to know if it exists.

Life is the highest good, and death the worst evil.

When people talk about a wealthy man of my creed they call him an Israelite; but if he is poor, they call him a Jew.

History is nothing but the soul's old wardrobe.

Beautiful women without religion are like flowers without perfume.

Advertising is necessary for business, and Life is a business like any other.

The instinct for grumbling of the rough and stiff-necked but honourable John Bull is perhaps the bulwark of British greatness abroad, and of British freedom at home.

Is poetry a disease of man, just as the pearl is only the material of a poor oyster's disease?

Perfumes are the feelings of flowers.

In Heaven roast geese fly round with gravy boats in their bills; tarts grow wild like sunflowers; everywhere there are brooks of bouillon and champagne; everywhere trees on which napkins flutter and you eat and wipe your lips and eat again without injury to your stomach. You sing psalms or flirt with the dear, delicate little angels.

> Graves, they say, are warmed by glory;
> Foolish words and empty story.

Experience is a good school, but the fees are high.

Silence – a conversation with an Englishman.

How strange! The very people who had given the world a God, and whose whole life was inspired by devotion to God, were stigmatised as deicides!

They praise the dramatist when he draws tears from an audience. The same talent is exhibited by the smallest onion.

Music played at weddings always reminds me of the music played for soldiers before they go off to battle.

Merchants throughout the world have the same religion.

We never converse willingly when talking is our profession.

Asked why he made a will on his deathbed leaving everything to his wife on condition she remarried after his death, Heine replied:

When Mathilda remarries, there will be at least one man who will regret my death.

Heine's famous last words. Asked on his deathbed if he thought God would forgive him:

Naturally, God will forgive me. That's His business.

*   *   *

Joseph Hergesheimer (1880-1954)
American novelist

No one can walk backward into the future.

* * *

Theodor Herzl (1860-1904)
Austrian journalist and founder of Political Zionism

A man who invents a terrible explosive does more for peace than a thousand wild apostles.

They will let you live only when you learn to die.

* * *

Samuel Hoffman
American writer

For every woman, who makes a fool out of a man, there is another woman, who makes a man out of a fool.

* * *

Samuel Hoffenstein (1890-1947)
American poet

> When I consider how we fret
> About a woman or a debt,
> And strive and strain and cark and cuss,
> And work and want and sweat and fuss,

And then observe the monkey swing
A casual tail at everything,
I am inclined to think that he
Evolved from apes like you and me.

No taxation without misrepresentation.

Marriages made in heaven are not exported.

Breathes there a man with hide so tough
Who says two sexes aren't enough?

The taste of another's luck is always tart.

The wages of sin are high.

The serpent has no feet or hands,
Yet makes his way in many lands;
But who would on his belly crawl
In order to avoid a fall.

Wherever the worm turns he is still a worm.

*   *   *

Leslie (Lord) Hore-Belisha (1893-1957)
Politician

On being called a 'little chit of a fellow' by his opponent during his first parliamentary election in 1922:

If you want a monument to the achievement of the older

politician you may find it across the Channel. It is three hundred miles long and half a mile deep, and it is studded with the tombstones of 'little chits of fellows'.

The Army is a part of the nation, not apart from the nation!

*   *   *

Moses Ibn Ezra (1070-1138)
Spanish-Hebrew philosopher

The biggest miser with his money is the biggest spend-thrift with his wishes.

The finest virtue in man is that of which he is unaware.

Love blinds us to faults, hatred to virtues.

Length is a mistake where brevity suffices.

Recipe for success:

I kept my mind awake, and my desires asleep.

*   *   *

Solomon Ibn Gabirol (1021-1069)
Spanish-Hebrew poet

Cast not pearls before swine, for they can do nothing with them.

To a fool silence is the best answer.

Worry over what has not occurred is a serious malady.

The best of animals need the whip, the purest of women a husband, and the cleverest of men to ask advice.

The test of good manners is being able to bear patiently with bad ones.

* * *

Isaac Goldberg (1887-1938)
American writer and critic

Snobbery is but a point in time. Let us have patience with our inferiors. They are ourselves of yesterday.

There is that smaller world which is the stage, and that larger stage which is the world.

Diplomacy is to do and say the nastiest things in the nicest way.

The trouble with most men of learning is that their learning goes to their heads.

Parody of 'My Country 'tis of Thee':

My grammar, 'tis of thee,
Sweet incongruity,

47

Of thee I sing.
I love each mood and tense,
Each freak of accidence,
Protect me from common sense,
Grammar, my King!

*   *   *

Abraham Ibn Hasdai (flourished around 1230)
Spanish-Hebrew author

Can pleasant words satisfy the hungry?

Gold comes from dust.

The wise man reports what he saw, the fool what he heard.

Rejoice in what you have;
don't sigh for what you lost.

Honeymoon for a month,
trouble for life.

Man has two ears and one tongue, so that he may listen more than he speaks.

*   *   *

Immanuel of Rome (1261-1330)
Hebrew poet (friend of Dante)

The best protection of a woman's virtue is a homely face.

A woman can dye her hair, but not change her character.

The burglar calls on divine aid while forcing the lock.

He who sows enmity reaps regret.

*   *   *

Rufus Isaacs (Marquis of Reading) (1860-1935)
Great lawyer and statesman

The Bar is never a bed of roses. It is either all bed and no roses, or all roses and no bed.

*   *   *

Vladimir Jabotinsky (1880-1940)
Author and Zionist pioneer

Well-chosen phrases are a great help in the smuggling of offensive ideas.

A Russian peasant once pronounced this mathematical theory: 'Four and four make eight, with this I can agree; some say that five and three make also eight – but that's a Jewish trick.'

*   *   *

49

Judah Jeiteles (1773-1838)
Austrian writer

Some friends are like a sun-dial, useless when the sun sets.

The miser does not own his wealth; his wealth owns him.

*   *   *

Franz Kafka (1883-1924)
Austrian novelist and playwright

Parents who expect gratitude from their children are like usurers who gladly risk their capital if only they receive interest.

*   *   *

Arthur Kober
American author

On his Confirmation Day:

I remember feeling a little like a combination of Lionel Strongfort and the doorman of the Russian Kretchma, the former because of the three watches (gifts) strapped to my wrists, and the latter because of the fountain pens (gifts) clasped to my coat-pocket like a series of cartridges in a Cossack's belt.

Bella, one of Kober's characters, on culture:

'S'posing a book is a big hit, then evveybody's reading it. Well, if evveybody's reading it, then right away the movies snap it up, it should be a pickcha. . . . I'll never forget the time I wasted reading *Gone with the Wind*. All I had to do was to hold tight a little while, then I would have seen it on the screen in one whole night insteada wasting God knows hommany weeks going through the book.'

*   *   *

Arthur Koestler
Novelist and essayist

Adolescence is a kind of emotional seasickness. Both are funny, but only in retrospect.

If you were to ask me what a writer's ambition should be, I would answer with a formula: to trade a hundred contemporary readers for ten readers in ten years and for one reader in a hundred years' time.

Palestine has the size of a county and the problems of a continent.

People don't mind if you betray humanity, but if you betray your club, you are considered a renegade.

Self-hatred is the Jew's patriotism.

*　　　*　　　*

Leopold Kompert (1822-1866)
Austrian ghetto novelist

God could not be everywhere, so He created mothers.

*　　　*　　　*

Levi (third century)
Palestinian sage and teacher

From his commentary on Genesis:

When God decided to create Eve, He considered from what part of Adam to create her. Said the Almighty: 'I will not use the head, lest she become conceited. I will not use the eyes, lest she be curious; nor the ear, lest she become an eavesdropper; nor the tongue, lest she be a gossip. I will not use the heart, lest she be jealous, nor the hand, lest she be grasping, nor the foot, lest she be a gadabout. I shall make her from a hidden part of man, so that even when she is naked it cannot be seen.'
God created Eve from one of Adam's ribs.
Alas, all the precautions were in vain. Woman is conceited, curious, a gossip, a chatterbox, she is jealous, grasping, and a gadabout.

*　　　*　　　*

Israel Lipkin (1810-1883)
Lithuanian scholar

A rabbi whom they don't want to drive out of town isn't a rabbi, and a rabbi whom they actually drive out isn't a man.

You need great talents to be a successful business man. If you have such talents, why waste them on business.

A small coin before the eyes will hide all from sight.

The tongue and the heart may be far apart, yet rain from the skies makes plants to rise.

The world is an expensive hotel; you pay dearly for each pleasure.

It is easy to write, it is hard to erase.

*   *   *

André Maurois (1885-1968)
French novelist and essayist

A man's variances are always explicable enough to himself.

Fame is worthless except as an offering of homage to those whom one loves.

53

To the disappointed man of ambition the world offer
sweet revenge. . . . In the eyes of women, the very fact o
an unplaced man's idleness is a merit, as it places him a
their services.

Modesty and unselfishness – these are the virtues me
praise – and pass by.

Long ago in London, I heard the story of the old gentle
man who, when buying a book for his daughter, timidl
asked: 'No sex in it, I hope?'
The saleswoman replied: 'No, sir, it's a love story.'

A true woman loves a strong man because she knows h
weaknesses.

*   *   *

Maimonides (Moses ben Maimon) (1135–1204)
Philosopher and physician

Astrology is a disease not a science.

A drowning man will catch at any rope.

Preachment is but babbling.

Plants bear witness to the reality of roots.

A sage is a greater asset to a nation than its King.

*   *   *

ord Mancroft

ndustrialist and politician

The most noticeable thing about Jews in politics is that they are so rarely noticeable.

Cricket is a game which the English, not being a spiritual people, have invented to give themselves some conception of eternity.

o a heckler with a very loud voice:

A man with your low intelligence should have a voice to match.

bout taking very young children abroad:

Never take a holiday that will end in tears.

I would rather people said 'Why has he stopped speaking?' than 'Why doesn't he?'

In all aspects of their business and professional life, women must be judged by their ability, not by using feminine tricks.

Happy is the man with a wife to tell him what to do, and a secretary to do it.

No man can consider himself truly married until he understands every word his wife is not saying.

When you are halfway through your speech sit down.

To Americans on Independence Day:

I will always regard July 4 as an English victory. English colonists with English traditions and English principles revolted against a German King – King George III – who employed Hessian mercenaries.

*   *   *

Mendele Mocher Sforim (1837-1917)
Mendele the bookseller, pen name of S J Abramowitz, Russian-Hebrew satirist

Better a Jew without a beard, than a beard without a Jew

Children without childhood are a dreadful sight.

Truth is a word each one understands as it suits him.

A pig is a pig, even when it plays a trick.

Who doesn't lie, can't be a marriage broker.

Pity was invented by the weak.

Money is the best advocate.

*   *   *

Benno Moisewitsch (1890-1963)
Eminent concert pianist

On gambling, of which he was fond:

The only way to double your money in a casino is to fold it and put it in your pocket.

With a piano I speak a universal language.

After an American tour:

America is God's own country. He's the only one who can afford to live there.

*   *   *

Ferenc Molnar (1878-1952)
Hungarian dramatist

To err gracefully is better than to guess the ugly truth.

Only man knows the agony of birth pangs.

Shakespeare was a genius, so let us merely strive to be honest.

*   *   *

57

THE WIT OF THE JEWS

George Jean Nathan (1882-1958)
American critic and essayist

Romantic love is the privilege of emperors, king
soldiers and artists; it is the butt of democrats, travelli
salesmen, magazine poets and the writers of Americ
novels.

Patriotism is often an arbitrary veneration of real est
above principles.

There is no such thing as a dirty theme. There are or
dirty writers.

The girl with the patient eardrum is the girl who fi
nabs a husband.

Criticism, in short, is simply and most often an attempt
reconcile personal prejudice with applied logic and t
deft concealment of what resulting gaps there may be
persuasive literary expression.

A man reserves his greatest and deepest love not for t
woman in whose company he finds himself electrifi
and enkindled, but for that one in whose company
may feel tenderly drowsy.

A man's wife is his compromise with the illusion of
first sweetheart.

*   *   *

Max Nordau (1849-1923)
physician and critic

The Englishman accepts a fit of delirium if it appears with footnotes, and is conquered by an absurdity if it is accompanied by diagrams.

Think of Disraeli; for whom any Jewish community would have been too confining, since the British Empire was hardly big enough for him.

*   *   *

S J Perelman
scriptwriter and essayist

On himself:

Button-cute, rapier-keen, wafer-thin and pauper poor, is S J Perelman, whose tall stooping figure is better known to the twilit half-world of five continents than to Publishers' Row. That he possesses the power to become invisible to finance companies; that his laboratory is tooled up to manufacture Frankenstein-type monsters on an incredible scale; and that he owns one of the rare mouths in which butter has never melted, are legends treasured by every schoolboy.

The effect of a film:

For six months after seeing Eric von Stroheim in *Foolish Wives,* I exhibited a maddening tendency to click my heels and murmur 'Bitte?', along with a twitch as though a monocle were screwed into my eye. The mannerism finally abated, but not until the Dean of Brown University had taken me aside and confided that if I wanted to transfer to Heidelberg, the faculty would not stand in my way.

Nowadays you don't know how much you know until your children grow up and tell you how much you don' know.

On Groucho Marx:

The picture was finished, and Groucho was at last free to resume his passionate avocation, the collecting and cross-fertilisation of various kinds of money.

Characterising a movie mogul:

In the words of a friend of mine, it was a case of, 'From Poland to Polo in one generation'.

*   *   *

Philo (20 BC–AD 40)
Alexandrian philosopher

Some who live are dead, and some who are dead still live

God bent the eyes of all other creatures downwards, but the eyes of man He set high, that he may behold Heaven

Flattery is friendship diseased.

It is the dark part of the eye that sees.

On ancestry:

If a man has lost the use of his eyes, will the keen sight of his ancestors help him to see?

*   *   *

Leo Pinsker (1821-1891)
Russian doctor and writer

The one thing most alien to men – humanity.

*   *   *

Elmer Rice (1892-1967)
American playwright

Man is a lazy animal. He works when he must: for bread to feed his body, or for approbation to feed his ego.

On slimming:

If Nature had intended our skeletons to be visible it would have put them on the outside of our bodies.

*   *   *

E

Anton Rubinstein (1830-1894)
Russian pianist and composer

For the Jews I am a Christian, for the Christians a Jew; for the Russians a German, for the Germans a Russian, for the classicists a futurist, for the futurists a retrograde. From this I conclude that I am neither fish nor meat – a sorrowful individual indeed!

The only letter which Englishmen write in capitals is I. This is the most-pointed comment on their national character.

*   *   *

Artur Rubinstein
World-famous pianist

Life means living, not escaping. I prefer to die young than to sniff around life.

When Rubinstein cancelled his Italian tour, because of the anti-semitic behaviour of the Government, and returned his decoration of the Order of the Commander of the Crown:

Mussolini said, 'What a shame! You lose so much money!' To which Rubinstein replied, 'Yes, but win so many hearts,' and signed himself 'Artur Rubinstein, Jewish Pianist.'

I accept life unconditionally. Most people ask for happiness on condition.

*　　　*　　　*

onas Edward Salk
Discoverer of anti-polio vaccine

Asked why he has devoted his life to research, he replied:

Why did Mozart compose music?

*　　　*　　　*

Herbert, Viscount Samuel, OM (1870-1963)
Statesman and philosopher

Sculpture is the art of thinking in shapes.

A library is like a garden – it needs constant pruning and weeding.

A library is thought in cold storage.

There are men of so much courage and independence that they would rather be in a minority and wrong, than right with the majority.

Do not choose to be wrong for the sake of being different.

63

The world is like a mirror: frown at it and it frowns you; smile, and it smiles too.

Equality of opportunity is an equal opportunity to prov unequal talents.

The future is more worth working for than the presen because there is so much more of it.

——'s long dull speech had only one redeeming feature that it was mostly inaudible.

The English spirit of compromise tempts us to believe th injustice, when it is halved, becomes justice.

The leader of a party must be someone who cares f something beyond the leadership of a party.

Life's taxi keeps on marking up its threepences, wheth you are driving anywhere or only sitting still.

We are here, not on a freehold, but on a tenancy; with maximum of a hundred years, but terminable at a time, with or without notice.

It takes two to make a marriage a success and only one failure.

Never waste good agony.

To have a friend be one.

Napoleon did supremely well many things that it was supremely ill to do.

We call it firmness when we agree, obstinacy when we don't.

He suffered occasionally from a rush of words to the head.

Some miss many pleasures through caring too much for comfort.

Possessing liberty, striving for equality, men forget fraternity, the greatest of the three.

On the Socialist State and human relations in industry:

You cannot expect much mother-love from an incubator.

The proof of the pudding is in the digesting.

It is not for the shouter to complain of the echo.

There are two sides to every question, because when there are no longer two sides it ceases to be a question.

It is easy to be tolerant of the principles of other people, if you have none of your own.

People who never do any work never have any holidays.

*   *   *

Moritz Saphir (1795-1858)
German writer

Nobody has a worse servant than he who is his own master.

Not every human being can be an author, but every author can be a human being.

Money and credit are curious things. Money is needed most when you don't have it, and credit you have most when you don't need it.

Life is the incurable disease from which all have so far died, and only those survive who are never born.

Saphir was a protégé of the Austrian Baron Rothschild, who gave an allowance to the writer:

One day, as he came for the usual stipend, Rothschild said jovially, 'Ah, Saphir. I see you've come for your money.' 'For *my* money?' retorted Saphir. 'No, Baron, you mean for *your* money.'

In order to become immortal, our great writers first have to die of hunger.

People do not kill time, time kills them.

Love makes a fool of the wisest man,
and a sage of the most foolish woman.

Love to a man, as to a magnet, has the greatest attraction only when it is combined with a certain metal.

Clever people are like fragrant roses; when you smell one rose it's delightful, but smelling a whole bouquet may give you a headache.

*   *   *

Arthur Schnitzler (1882-1931)
Austrian dramatist and novelist

One can positively never be deceived if one mistrusts everything in the world, even one's own scepticism.

Sentimentality is feeling acquired below cost.

It is easy to write memoirs when one has a poor memory.

No one is poorer than the rich who doesn't know how to spend.

*   *   *

Haim Schwarzbaum
Israeli author

A fellow is standing in the street, engrossed in thoughts. A friend asks him, 'What are you thinking about?' He replies, 'I'm contemplating a queer phenomenon. I think I'm a rather strange animal. The King of the animals is the lion. The bear is afraid of the lion, the wolf fears the bear, the dog fears the wolf, the cat fears the dog, the reptile fears the mouse, my wife is afraid of the mouse, and I fear my wife. . . . Imagine what queer animal I am!'

*   *   *

Sholom Aleichem (Sholom Rabinowitz) (1859–1916)

Yiddish humorist. The great musical success 'Fiddler on the Roof' was based on his stories of Tevye the Milkman

To want to be the cleverest of all is the biggest folly.

The luckiest man was Adam – he had no mother-in-law.

Barking dogs don't bite, but they themselves don't know it.

A pretty face is half a dowry.

Fritters in a dream are not fritters, but a dream.

Better the bite of a friend than the kiss of an enemy.

The more poverty, the more hope.

Men are divided into two categories, scabs and scabs. If you have no money you're obviously a scab, and if you have money, you're certainly a scab, otherwise you wouldn't have money.

A miserly man and a fat cow are only useful when they're dead.

Was pretty, *had* money, *could* sing – all these are absolutely useless.

A wise word is no substitute for a piece of herring or a bag of oats.

If a horse with four legs can stumble, how much more a man with one tongue.

God must hate a poor man, else why did He make him poor.

If you have money you are wise, and beautiful, and you can sing.

You know when a fool speaks – he grinds much and produces little.

Lawyers are like doctors. What one says the other contradicts.

Life: a drama for the wise, a game for the fool, a comedy for the rich, a tragedy for the poor.

You don't have to be big to be great.

Dear God – I know we are your chosen people, but couldn't you choose some other people for a change?

* * *

Baruch Spinoza (1632-1677)
Dutch philosopher

The world would be much happier if men were as fully able to keep silence as they are able to speak.

Everyone has as much right as he has might.

What Paul says about Peter tells us more about Paul than about Peter.

*   *   *

Joshua Steinberg (1839-1908)
Russian author

Glorying in ancestors is like searching for fruit among the roots.

An ass is known by his big ears, a fool by his big tongue.

*   *   *

Alfred Sutro (1863-1933)
Playwright

Modesty is one of the seven deadly virtues.

They say that there are sixty-seven different ways in which a woman can like a man.

He suffers from chronic indecision. He's like a snail that has had his licence endorsed.

*   *   *

Chaim Weizmann (1874-1952)
Eminent chemist and first President of Israel

Miracles sometimes occur, but one has to work terribly hard for them.

You will always be treated as a guest if you, too, can play the host. The only man who is invited to dinner is the man who can have dinner at home if he likes.

We are perhaps the sons of dealers in old clothes, but we are the grandsons of prophets.

The world is divided into two groups of nations – those that want to expel the Jews and those that do not want to receive them.

I do not consider it a compliment to be called 'the salt of the earth'. Salt is used for someone else's food. It dissolves in that food. And salt is good only in small quantities. If there is too much salt in the food you throw out the food and the salt with it.

Conversations and negotiations with Arabs are not unlike chasing a mirage in the desert: full of promise and good to look at, but likely to lead you to death by thirst.

The walls of Jericho fell to the sound of shouts and trumpets. I never heard of walls being raised by that means.

*   *   *

Vera Weizmann (1881-1966)
Wife of Israel's first President

We Jews are strange people: we remember Moses, King David, and Solomon, but we know little of our own ancestry beyond our parents, and occasionally our grandparents.

Quoting her husband:

Difficult things take a long time, the impossible takes a little longer.

*   *   *

Stephen S Wise (1874-1949)
American rabbi

I would rather think of my religion as a gamble than to think of it as an insurance premium.

*   *   *

Humbert Wolfe (1885-1940)
English poet

From his ABC of the Theatre:

C is the censor. He keeps the stage clean by ruling out God and the Crown as obscene.

I is the Ighbrows. The pain in their neck was caused by the keyhole when studying sex.

Q is the queue. How enchanting to sit in a blizzard all day, and then faint in the pit.

T is Tallulah. She was rightly annoyed when a journalist called her the Helen of Freud.

Illiteracy is a form of curable blindness.

*   *   *

Herman Wouk
American scholar and novelist

Income tax returns are the most imaginative fiction being written today.

*   *   *

Israel Zangwill (1864-1926)
Novelist and playwright

The only true love is love at first sight; second sight dispels it.

73

The average taxpayer is no more capable of a 'grand passion' than of a grand opera.

If there were no Jews they would have to be invented for the use of politicians – they are indispensable, the antithesis of a panacea; guaranteed to *cause* all evils.

No man is a hero to his valet – or his relatives.

'Bolshevism' is one of those words which people put into their mouth to steal away their brains.

All Jews should set up a statue to Lenin for not being a Jew.

For the actor, despite Euclid, the part is greater than the whole.

Their only ability was respectability.

Fortunately, religion depends as little upon theology as love upon phrenology.

To destroy capital you need a capitalist.

On the road of life there is no returning.

What can be more digestive after a good dinner than a spirited denunciation of the sinfulness of eating it.

To save people leaders must be lost.

Psychoanalysis! That's indecency reduced to science!

Philosophy – All my I.
Art – All my eye.
Religion – All my Ay.

Fools follow rules, wise men precede them.

After all, what is love? In lawn-tennis it counts for nothing.

Looking backward is a luxury which should be indulged in only in moderation – say once in fifty years.

We learn only from our own mistakes, and when it is too late to profit by them.

The keenest joys of the senses leave a scant deposit in the memory.

> Wherefore do the critics rage?
> 'Tis the Biographic Age.
> Every dolt who duly died
> In a book is glorified.
> Uniformly with his betters;
> All his unimportant letters
> Edited by writers gifted,
> Every scrap of MS sifted,

> Classified by dates and ages,
> Pages multiplied on pages,
> Till the man is – for their pains –
> Buried 'neath his own Remains

The true-hero nowadays is the man who conquers himself and does not write books.

Selfishness is the only real atheism.

Indifference and hypocrisy between them keep orthodoxy alive.

Let us start a new religion with one commandment 'Enjoy thyself'.

There's no narrower creature in the world than your idealist, he sets up a moral standard which suits his own line of business, which rails at men of the world for not conforming to it.

Most religious folks do their moral book-keeping by double entry.

*   *   *

Leopold Zunz (1794-1866)
German scholar

Certain virtues are always fashionable, but not virtue.

Ideas are duty free.

Give bread to a dog, oil to a door, blows to a quarreler, and board to a scoffer, and you will silence all four.

Show Business

Larry Adler
Harmonica virtuoso

Music shouldn't really be put in cans, it tends to spoil.

*   *   *

David Belasco (1853-1931)
American actor, playwright and theatrical manager

When I can think more with my head and less with my heart, the world will think me wise – and I shall know myself a fool.

The eyes of the heart see quickly and judge rightly.

We must not waste time for that's the stuff life's made of.

For women marriage is the greatest of all careers: therefore do not try to mix any of the others with it.

*   *   *

Jack Benny
World-famous TV, stage and screen star

I might have been a fairly good violinist, maybe the second best. But who cares about the second best? This way it's fine. I'm the world's worst violinist.

Commenting on his violin:

If it isn't a Stradivarius, I've been robbed of a hundred and ten dollars.

On his first radio appearance in 1932:

Ladies and Gentlemen, this is Jack Benny. There will be now a brief pause while everyone says 'Who cares?'

In Benny's press cuttings:

Jack Benny played Mendelssohn last night. Mendelssohn lost.

The joke that gained Benny his loudest laugh:

A robber says: 'Your money or your life.'
Benny pauses and finally replies: 'I'll have to think it over.'

Before your fortieth birthday keep circulating the story that you're thirty-nine. If people hear it often enough they'll believe it for years.

*   *   *

Milton Berle
American comedian and writer

My Philosophy of Life: Life is very simple. The first thing to remember about life is – don't worry about it. Really, there are only two things to worry about; either you're successful or you're not successful. If you're successful there's nothing to worry about. If you're not successful there's only two things to worry about; if your health is good there's nothing to worry about. If your health is bad there's only two things to worry about. Either you're going to live or you're not going to live. If you live there's nothing to worry about, and if you don't live, why you've only two things to worry about. Either you're going to heaven or you're not going to heaven. If you go to heaven there's nothing to worry about, and if you go to the other place, you'll be so doggone busy shaking hands with all your old friends, YOU WON'T HAVE TIME TO WORRY.

*   *   *

Fanny Brice (1891-1951)
American stage star

I never loved a man I liked, and never liked a man I loved.

*   *   *

George Burns
Famous as the partner of the late Gracie Allen, in their renowned 'dizzy' act

They named me Nathan Birnbaum. When I was born I was the youngest in my family, but this position didn't last long. There were more to come. Before Mother got through there were twelve.

People think all I have to do is to stand up and tell a few jokes. Well, that's not as easy as it looks. Every year it gets to be more of an effort to stand up.

'Lucky is the man who knows his limitations.' I know mine. That's why I hire so many capable people who can do the job I'm not capable of doing.

You never work so hard as when you're not being paid for it.

*　　　*　　　*

Eddie Cantor (1892–1964)
Famous American comedian

My father was the first man to sell blarney stones from a push-cart.

Arguing with a woman is like going into a shower bath with an umbrella. What good does it do?

We call our rich relatives the kin we love to touch.

A girl in good shape is often the reason why a man is in bad shape.

If you advertised for a mother, do you know how the ad would read? WANTED: A WOMAN TO COOK AND SEW, TO CLEAN HOUSE, WASH CLOTHES, AND DO ALL THE ODD JOBS IN BETWEEN. MUST BE AT HOME WITH ILLNESS, ADVERSITY, AND CRISIS OF EVERY KIND. NO SALARY, NO VACATION, NO CHANCE FOR ADVANCEMENT!
Now you know that nobody would ever answer an ad like that. That's why God invented mothers.

Lust isn't all there is to sex. Sex isn't all there is to love. But love is almost all there is to life. . . . Love isn't like a reservoir – you'll never drain it dry. . . . Love/live. Switch a single letter and they're just the same.

The two most common causes of divorce? – Men and women.

*   *   *

Alma Cogan (1933-1966)
Popular singer

I'm very ambitious! My head comes before my heart.

Some people go to a psychiatrist, others get married.

In my business marriage is difficult. In any case I buy my own minks.

*   *   *

Sammy Davis Jr
Reputed to be the world's finest entertainer

Asked what his handicap is:

I'm a coloured one-eyed Jew – do I need anything else?

The world doesn't hate losers, it just has no time for them.

To a heckler:

If you're ever in California, sir, I do hope you'll come by and use my pool – I'd love to give you some drowning lessons!

The guys who wrote the history books happened to be white, and by a strange coincidence they managed to overlook just about everything any Negro did in and for America, except pull barges up the goddamned Mississippi.

*   *   *

Bernard Delfont
Stage and screen impresario

Asked questions about the film industry:

What I'm doing is listening. I'm the best listener you have ever heard.

*   *   *

Brian Epstein (1935-1967)
Brought the Beatles to fame

On popularity:

> Everyone likes to matter, but it can go too far. One begins to feel like a goldfish, swimming round and round to help other people relax.

> Once the wives of the Beatles start talking to the Press, their whole lives become a comedy.

*   *   *

Bud Flanagan (1896-1968)
'Clown Prince to the Royal Family'

Standing in the wings at a Royal Command performance, and watching a troupe of acrobats doing miraculous somersaults and 'beating themselves to death', he was heard to murmur:

> Look at those silly so-and-so's, too lazy to learn a comic song.

Receiving the OBE at Buckingham Palace, he said to Prince Philip:

> You've got a smashing house here for a matinée.

After saying something 'saucy' at a royal luncheon:

They can't put me in the Tower while the tourist season is on.

The brand-new original joke is as rare as a pop singer who can sing.

If Prince Philip would let his hair grow I could get him in with the Rolling Stones. He is the working girl's Adam Faith. He is as sophisticated as Noël Coward, as charming as Chevalier, and as versatile as the Governor of Pentonville Prison.

I would lay down a million lives for our grand royal couple . . . and if that doesn't get me a knighthood I don't know what will.

Show business is ninety-eight per cent luck and two per cent talent.

*   *   *

Daniel Frohman (1851-1940)
American theatrical impresario

I believe in all religions, especially if they are of whole cloth, not shoddy or threadbare. Beside the various religions are only different forms of fire insurance.

Can you imagine what the life of Adam and Eve must have been in the Garden of Eden before the apple episode? The inescapable monotony of their existence.

Eve put up the job about the apple. What was the result
They were fired out of the Garden of Eden. Adam got
job and went to work. Eve got some clothes to wear, an
when they met at night, they had something to talk abou

*   *   *

George Gershwin (1899-1937)
Famous American composer

Originality is the only thing that counts.

Never rely on inspiration. When we want it most,
never comes.

On his mother:

She is wonderful, and so modest about me.

*When he was told that the girl he hoped to marry had eloped wi
someone else:*

I'd feel terrible about this if I were not so busy.

*   *   *

Samuel Goldwyn
Famous film producer

Many of the sayings (Goldwynisms) attributed to Mr Goldw

*e doubtless apocryphal. Goldwyn has often wished that he were
art enough to say the things with which he is credited.

o a man who admired Mrs Goldwyn's hands:

Yes, I'm going to have a bust made of them.

*o a friend who said that Goldwyn's new film would be a
nmercial hit:

To hell with that. I don't care if it never makes a cent. All
I want is for everybody to go and see it.

is line on publicity:

Say what you like about me – as long as you spell the
name right.

I read part of it all the way through.

That's the way with these directors, they're always biting
the hand that lays the golden egg.

Excuse me, I am going out for some tea and trumpets.

The sweetness of low budget never equals the bitterness of
low quality.

I'll give you a definite maybe.

Include me out.

I can answer you in two words: im-possible.

Anyone who goes to a psychiatrist ought to have his head examined.

That atomic bomb – it's dynamite.

A verbal agreement isn't worth the paper it's written on.

A wide screen just makes a bad film twice as bad.

The trouble with this business is the dearth of bad pictures.

*　　　*　　　*

Sir Lew Grade
Television tycoon

As with Samuel Goldwyn many of the stories attributed to Sir Lew Grade are certainly apocryphal.

When he was an agent:

The trouble with this business is that the stars keep ninety per cent of my money.

Small child: What does two times two make?
Lew Grade: Buying or selling?

n ATV Golden Hour of Entertainment:

Culture? This is the greatest thing that's ever happened in Culture. We have everybody: Callas, Picasso, Barenboim, Stradivarius . . .

I've succeeded in the business by knowing exactly what I hate.

*　　*　　*

aurence Harvey
reen and stage star

Some of my best moments are spent with me.

n women:

Dealing with them is rather like dealing with a known thief. Always remember that the people who sat around the guillotine knitting were women.

*　　*　　*

eorge Jessel
oastmaster General of US'. Famous comedian

eaking in support of Roosevelt:

I know Governor Thomas E Dewey (Roosevelt's oppo-nent), and Mr Dewey is a fine man. (*A hushed pause.*) Yes,

Dewey is a fine man. So is my Uncle Morris. My Unc[le]
Morris shouldn't be President; neither should Dewey.

More than once I have heard the prominent citizen, wh[o]
is being honoured, magnanimously give all the credit f[or]
his success to 'the little woman, who shared my ups-an[d]
downs, and been my great inspiration etc etc.'
Too often, later, I've seen him put the missus in the car [to]
go home alone, while he 'returns to the office'.

The widow of a friend of mine decided to sell her la[te]
husband's new Cadillac for forty dollars.
'Why,' I asked her, 'are you selling this beautiful car [so]
cheap?' 'I'll tell you why,' she replied. 'In my husban[d's]
last will he asked that this Cadillac be sold and t[he]
proceeds be given to his beautiful young secretary. I a[m]
following his wishes – to the letter. With the commissi[on]
and the tax deducted, she'll get just about ten dollars.'

After a flowery introduction by a speaker:

That was a beautiful speech; for a moment I though[t I]
was dead.

When the Friars honoured Jessel for fifty years in show busine[ss:]

It may be true that life begins at forty, but after fifty ye[ars]
it's only from the waist up.

Public speaking is like drilling for oil; if you don't stri[ke]
it in three minutes, stop boring!

Don't tell a girl you're tired unless it's of her.

*　　　*　　　*

Al Jolson (1886–1950)
American stage and screen star

I travelled with a Jew (in the SS *Leviathan*) who thought that the ship's name was 'Levi-Nathan'.

A 'classy' hotel is a place where they say 'Guess what the bill is', and you guess wrong.

A thousand Nubian maidens, dressed only in long hair, attended the funeral of an Egyptian King.
That was to prove that he was dead.

In Hollywood I played poker with the film magnates. I played for about a minute, because they regard ten thousand dollars as tissue paper.

*　　　*　　　*

Danny Kaye
Stage, TV and screen star

If there is a dispute between a musician and myself it is settled amicably. I win.

*　　　*　　　*

Jerome Kern (1885-1945)
Great popular composer

If you wait for inspiration to light on your shoulder and
gently poke cobwebs from your brain you had better
change your profession. . . . You get a nibble and you
don't know whether it is a minnow or a marlin until
you reel it in.

On trying out a song:

I play it for my wife. If she doesn't like it, I know I have
a hit on my hands.

*To an actress, who kept rolling her 'r's' all the time, and said to
Kern, 'You want me to cr–r–r–r–r–ross the stage. How can I get
acr–r–r–r–oss?' Answered Kern:*

My dear, why don't you just roll on your r-r-r-s?

*　　　*　　　*

Fritz Kortner
German stage and screen star

*In answer to younger people telling him that he could not under-
stand their problems, he replied:*

You were never as old as I am, on the other hand I was
as young as you are now.

*　　　*　　　*

rnst Lubitsch (1892–1947)
amous film director

*ubitsch heard that film producer Daryl Zanuck is alleged to have
id that after inspecting the Mona Lisa fifty times he could see
thing special in it.*

o which Lubitsch replied:

There are three pictures I would like to have. The Mona
Lisa, a picture of Zanuck looking at the Mona Lisa, and
a picture of the Mona Lisa looking at Zanuck.

is definition of the Jewish Curse:

You should have a lot of money, but you should be the
only one in your family with it.

*writer boasted that he had all the gems of literature in his
rary. Answered Lubitsch:*

Uncut, no doubt.

Writers are more wage conscious than story conscious.

The wages of cynicism are worse than death.

It's better to live rich than to die rich.

*   *   *

Wolf Mankowitz
Playwright and author

Auctions are an exploitative technique designed to make people pay more than an object is worth.

Referring to his failure to receive a British Oscar for one of his films:

You can definitely say that my gall isn't divided in three parts.

On hearing that Lord Boothby is to play himself in a documentary:

He's been playing the part all his life. He should be pretty good by now.

Some Mankowitz definitions:

ACTOR-PROOF: A play so brilliant that no actor can harm it.

ELOCUTION: A common substitute for acting ability.

IMPRESARIO: Flattery for managers who like to think of themselves as creating the climate in which great enterprises of show business grow, blossom, and come to fruit as cash and kudos.

*   *   *

Groucho (Julius Henry) Marx
World-famous comedian

When a person starts writing his memoirs it's a sure sign he's washed up!

Comment on the first London reception of the Marx Brothers:

It was so silent in the theatre that you'd have thought we were playing *Hamlet*.

When the audience threw pennies on the stage, Groucho addressed them:

We don't mind being insulted, but if you must throw coins, how about throwing something that'll do us some good – like shillings and guineas.

When I was a young boy I used to think that if you were very nice to very rich people they would give you fabulous presents, like a Cadillac or a house on the French Riviera. But as I journeyed through life I discovered that rich people give you nothing – that's why they're rich. So now I insult them all I want.

Asked if he wouldn't like to be his son's age and start life all over again:

'I can't think of a more revolting idea. I've been through life once and that's enough for me.
'Not even for a million dollars?'

95

'Well, maybe for a million dollars, but it would have to be all tax free.'

On being accused of being obsessed with sex:

It's not an obsession, it's a talent.

Speaking of his father who was a tailor:

He was known as Misfit-Sam. As his reputation grew, he was forced to go further from home to snare new victims.

On being examined to become an air-raid warden:

'If you went home and found your wife's head in the oven with the gas turned on – what would you do?'
'That's simple,' answered Groucho, 'I'd baste her every fifteen minutes.'

I wouldn't join a club that would have me as a member.

I never forget a face, but in your case I'll make an exception.

There's one way to find out if a man is honest – ask him. If he says 'yes', you know he's crooked.

Groucho in a letter to Sam Zolotow:

My plans are still in embryo. In case you've never been

there, this is a small town on the outskirts of wishful thinking.

. . *to Irving Hoffman:*

Between strokes of good fortune, I have been toying with the idea of making you my impending child's god-father. However, before doing this officially, I would like to see a notarised statement of your overall assets.

. . *to Phil Silvers:*

Marry, if you must, but don't marry a chorus girl. No matter where you take them, they order champagne and chicken à la king. This can be very embarrassing if you are in the Automat.

However, if you must marry, I suggest you look in other fields. In a city as big as New York I am sure there are pants manufacturers, wholesale delicatessen dealers, and various other merchants who have daughters, who conceivably have virtues even more indispensable to a near-sighted major comic than a talent for high kicking.

So look smart, be smart, and remember . . . in union there is alimony.

. . *To the Lunts:*

I thought I would be able to take you up on your kind invitation. Luckily for you, I won't be able to come. You have no idea how fortunate you are, because I'm particularly loathsome guest and I eat like a vulture. Unfortunately, the resemblance doesn't end here.

... *to Eddie Cantor:*

The two biggest laughs I can recall (other than my thre marriages) were in a vaudeville act called 'Home again' One was when Zeppo came out from the wings an announced, 'Dad, the garbage man is here.' I replied 'Tell him we don't want any.'
The other was when Chico shook hands with me an said: 'I would like to say good-bye to your wife,' and said, 'Who wouldn't.'

... *to Arthur Sheekman:*

I have just read in the *Reporter* that Irving Berlin's bite o of his last two pictures was 1,300,000 dollars. Is it ar wonder he keeps singing, 'There's no business like Sho Business?' There is also no business man like Irving Berli Not that I begrudge him this. He is a giant talent wor every nickel he gets. Single-handed, if he were intereste I believe he could pay off the British debt.

I have no advice to give to young struggling actors. ¹ young, struggling actresses, my advice is to keep stru gling. If you struggle long enough you will never get trouble and if you never get in trouble, you will never much of an actress.

From Groucho's column in 'Variety':

As for marriage, I know hundreds of husbands who would gladly go home if there weren't any wives waiting for them. Take the wives out of marriage and there wouldn't be any divorces.

But then, someone might ask, what about the next generation?

Look, I've seen some of the next generation – perhaps it's just as well if the whole thing ends right here.

*   *   *

Paul Muni (1895-1967)
American stage and screen star

The man who never made an enemy never made anything.

*   *   *

Rachel (Elisa Rachel Felix) (1821-1858)
Famous French actress

On why she would not marry one of her many lovers:

I am very willing to have lodgers, but not proprietors.

*   *   *

Billy Rose (1899–1966)
Fabulous American showman

On his first book:

To give it tone and class, it's being brought out in a limited edition – limited to people with three dollars.

I was born the night President McKinley was shot, and a lot of fellows around Broadway will tell you they shot the wrong man.

I wrote the first singing commercial: There, I've said it and I'm glad. For years I've been walking around with this secret, fraternising with people who are kind to small animals and bathe every day. Now I've come clean.

In 1928 I persuaded the great comedienne (Fanny Brice) to become Mrs Rose. The day she did, I automatically became known as Mr Brice.

I'd like to sneak into the Hall of Fame some night and chop up most of the statues. You can't make me believe that Hiram Maxim, inventor of the machine gun, rate a thousand pounds of bronze.

After the manner of the famous will which left the fields to small boys and the stars to lovers, I'll tack on the following codicils:
To Audiences – A theatre architect who knows the differences between a lobby and a telephone booth.

To Understudies – The plagues of Egypt to wish upon the leads an hour before curtain time.

To Showgirls – A line of dialogue and a set of theatrical offices without divans.

To Chorus Girls – The report of the American Wild Life Society on the preservation of the mink.

To Midtown Restaurants – A coffee cup that bites waiters' thumbs.

On giving:

If a guy is trying to melt down a girl who carries a jeweller's eye-piece in her bag, he's in trouble. Either he gets himself a machine that prints money, or he gets a new wife.

*   *   *

Joe Schenk (1878-1961)
Film industry pioneer

In a capital of atheism like Hollywood what can a man believe in.

*   *   *

Barbra Streisand
American screen and stage star

Commenting on a scene in the film 'Funny Girl', when she, a Jewess, is kissed by Omar Sharif, an Egyptian:

Never mind what Nasser will say! You should have heard what my Aunt Rosie said!

Superstar? It's just a title, a word. I don't understand all that bull.

Asked about the millions she may earn:

You can't eat more than one pastrami-on-rye sandwich at a time.

*   *   *

Michael Todd (1909-1958)
Famous American impresario

Illusion is the first of pleasures, and no tree in the world is as beautiful as the tree in your mind.

Money is only important if you haven't got it.

To an unsympathetic request:

How do you want your no, fast or slow?

Poverty is a state of mind. When you start thinking with your wallet, you're always wondering what you can't do instead of what you can do and you're never going to get off your back.

Life is a toy balloon among children armed with pins.

If a man does not know what is impossible, he will do it.

*   *   *

Chaim Topol
Israeli stage and screen star

In our country we don't believe in miracles. We *rely* on them.

About the English:

Very tolerant people. For a foreigner to live in London is very comfortable – I hope it's the same for an Englishman!

*   *   *

Billy Wilder
American writer and film director

On his films:

My pictures are not intended to reform people; hopefully they are stories sufficiently intriguing to make them forget the popcorn.

There are some I loathe less than others.

On critics:

What they call dirty in our pictures they call lusty in foreign films.

They object not to the vulgarity in my art, but the lack of art in my vulgarity.

On TV – 'The 21 inch Prison':

I'm delighted with that medium, because it used to be that we in films were – the lowest form of art. Now we have something to look down on.

To his wife when courting her:

I'd worship the ground you walk on if you lived in a better neighbourhood.

In 1945 Billy Wilder was with the US Army Psychological Warfare Division:

After the war, some Germans wanted to put on a Passion Play, and a carpenter wrote me asking permission to play Jesus. After we screened them, we found that six of the Apostles were Gestapo men, and the carpenter a storm trooper. I said, 'Yes, as long as the nails are real.'

Years ago I wanted to make a movie on the career of the great ballet star Nijinsky, who ended his days in a Swiss asylum believing himself to be a horse. I took the idea to

Sam Goldwyn and even before explaining the story I knew all was lost.

'Have you gone crazy?' Goldwyn said. 'You want to make a picture about a man who thinks he's a horse?'

'Well,' I said at the door, 'we could always have a happy ending, we could show him winning the Derby.'

Finance

A Jewish banker had framed above his desk: 'Every favour has its revenge.'

*   *   *

Bernard M Baruch (1870–1965)
American statesman and financier

An elder statesman is somebody old enough to know his own mind and keep quiet about it.

The terror created by weapons has never stopped men from employing them.

We must remember that the people do not belong to the government, but that the governments belong to the people.

There are no such things as incurables; there are only things for which man has not found a cure.

On his eighty-fifth birthday:

To me old age is always fifteen years older than I am.

Age is only a number, a cipher for the records. A man can't retire his experience. He must use it. Experience achieves more with less energy and time.

Advice to business men on health:

Always do one thing less than you think you can do.

Beware of him who promises something for nothing.

The art of living lies less in eliminating our troubles than in growing with them.

On society:

What's the use of wearing yourself out in the evening talking to people who don't know anything.

The stock market is people trying to read the future.

*   *   *

Viscount Bearsted (1853-1927)
Founder of Shell Oil Co.

Nothing sells itself.

Success is not on the beaten path.

*   *   *

Otto Kahn (1867-1934)
American banker and philanthropist

To young business men:

Eliminate from your vocabulary in working hours the word 'perfunctory'.

The most serviceable of all assets is reputation.

Consider one of the essential requisites of your diet a supply of the milk of human kindness. To be hard-headed one does not have to be 'hard-boiled'.

Those who love art and are truly susceptible to its spell, do die young in the sense that they remain young to their dying day.

Too often art emerging from the garrets, in the plentitude of strength and promise, has been undone in palaces.

*   *   *

Solomon Loeb (1867-1933)
Banker

Always say NO, first. I have become a millionaire by saying NO.

*   *   *

THE ROTHSCHILDS

*As is customary with great families, a web of myth has been spun
around the Rothschilds, and historians and writers differ in attrib-
uting stories to any particular member of the family.
We have attempted to keep the record as faithful as possible.*

Güttle (1753-1849)
Wife of Mayer Amschel, founder of the House of Rothschild

When a guest observed on her ninety-fourth birthday that
she would outlive them all, she replied in the stock-
market language of her sons: 'Why should God take me
at a hundred, when he can have me at ninety-four?'

*   *   *

Amschel Mayer (1773-1855)

To an anti-semitic crowd besieging his house in Frankfurt:

My friends, you want money from the rich Jew. There are
forty million Germans. I have about as many florins. As a
beginning I'll drop a florin to each of you.

The mob held out their hands, caught the money, and left.

*   *   *

H

Nathaniel Mayer (1777-1836)
Founder of the London House

Asked by his small son how many nations there were in the world:

There are only two to worry about, there is the Family, and there are the others.

To a very important person shouting his grievance, Nathaniel, busy over some papers, said, 'Take a chair'. The important one then shouted about his noble lineage: 'Take two chairs,' said Rothschild.

*   *   *

Lord Rothschild (1840-1915)

Asked if there was a recipe for making money in the stock-market:

There is. It consists of selling too soon.

If one does anybody a good turn it is generally a question of getting shelter somewhere from their abuse.

It isn't enough to love money, it is also necessary for money to love you.

To the driver of a hansom cab, who looked askance at a tip from Lord Rothschild, and remarked that his lordship's son gave twice as much, Rothschild said:

I know, my son has a millionaire for a father; I haven't.

*　　　*　　　*

Lord Rothschild

Asked by Dr Weizmann, during World War II, why he had not sent his children to the United States, Lord Rothschild replied:

Because of their name. If I sent those three little things over there the world would say that seven million Jews are cowards.

*　　　*　　　*

James de Rothschild (1878-1957)

I never had a chance to earn half-a-crown in my life. If I had had that chance, I might have become a great man.

*　　　*　　　*

Joseph Seligman (1819-1880)
Financier

Began as a pedlar in America and founded a great family fortune.

Money earns money even while you sleep.

*　　　*　　　*

James Seligman
Brother of Joseph

To sell something you have, to someone who wants it – that is not business. But to sell something you don't have to someone who doesn't want it – *that* is business.

*   *   *

Sir Isaac Wolfson, Bart.
Philanthropist and head of a vast business empire

My filing system is my brain and my waste-paper basket.

From Sages Through the Ages

These witticisms have been gathered from the Talmud, the Apocrypha, and from Yiddish literature.

Words should be weighed, not counted.

*   *   *

Learn to be a barber on someone else's beard.

*   *   *

Lend money and you acquire an enemy.

*   *   *

If the heart is bitter, sugar in the mouth won't help.

*   *   *

Small children, small joys; big children, big annoys.

*   *   *

Don't go to market just with wisdom.

*   *   *

Give your ear to everybody, your hand to your friends, but your lips only to your wife.

*   *   *

If you lie with dogs you get up with fleas.

*   *   *

The eye is small but it sees the world.

*   *   *

In hell an ox is worth a farthing, but nobody has that farthing.

*   *   *

You can't chew with somebody else's teeth.

*   *   *

Better to talk to a woman and think of God, than to talk to God and think of a woman.

*   *   *

Tears don't liquidate debts.

*   *   *

Tell a secret to a woman, but cut off her tongue.

*   *   *

Where there's honey, there are flies.

*   *   *

Love tastes sweet, but only with bread.

*   *   *

Better an ounce of luck, than a pound of gold.

*   *   *

When a poor man eats chicken one of them is sick.

*   *   *

A man should live if only to satisfy his curiosity.

*   *   *

A fool grows without rain.

*   *   *

Your health comes first – you can always hang yourself later.

* * *

If you can't bite show your teeth.

* * *

God never told anyone to be stupid.

* * *

God loves the poor and helps the rich.

* * *

'For dust thou art and unto dust thou shalt return' – in between a drink comes in handy.

* * *

Shrouds have no pockets.

* * *

Much knowledge ages you – much money makes you feel young.

* * *

If you rub elbows with a rich man, you get a hole in your sleeve.

*   *   *

God gives nothing for nothing.

*   *   *

When an ox falls men sharpen their knives.

*   *   *

You can't get two skins off one ox.

*   *   *

If a Jew breaks a leg, he thanks God he did not break both legs; if he breaks both, he thanks God that he did not break his neck.

*   *   *

The longest distance is to the pocket.

*   *   *

The sun will set without your assistance.

*   *   *

117

When is a pauper miserable? When he is invited to two weddings in one day.

*   *   *

'Lots of property, lots of headache' – but no property at all, that's even a greater headache.

*   *   *

When a son gets married, he gives his wife a contract, and his mother a divorce.

*   *   *

A liar must have a good memory.

*   *   *

Rich relations are close relations; poor relations are distant relations.

*   *   *

You can't dance at two weddings at the same time; nor can you sit on two horses with one behind.

*   *   *

The soldiers fight, and the Kings are heroes.

*   *   *

Poverty comes from God, but not dirt.

*   *   *

The egg of today is better than the hen of tomorrow.

*   *   *

Money makes even bastards legitimate.

*   *   *

Money is round so it rolls away.

*   *   *

A stale crust is more useful to the poor man than a lot of fresh air.

*   *   *

Life is the cheapest bargain – you get it for nothing.

*   *   *

It's better to be dead drunk than dead hungry.

*   *   *

Silence is restful. It gives rest to the heart, the larynx, the tongue, the lips and the mouth.

*   *   *

The best part about telling the truth is that you don't have to remember what you said.

*   *   *

Those who have nothing are always eager to share it with others.

*   *   *

You may not be here tomorrow, and you will have worried about a world which is not yours.

*   *   *

When a divorced man marries a divorced woman there are four minds in the bed.

*   *   *

A bride with beautiful eyes need not worry about her figure.

*   *   *

Of ten measures of gossip that came into the world, woman took nine.

*   *   *

Why are the fingers fashioned like pegs? So that if a man hears anything unworthy, he may plug his ears.

*   *   *

Why is a man more easily pacified than a woman? Because man was made out of earth, and woman out of a hard rib.

*   *   *

A good wife is half an income.

*   *   *

Don't question the ways of Providence, because the Lord may say: If you are so anxious for an answer come up to me.

*   *   *

Beware of borrowing money from a poor man, or kissing an ugly maid.

*   *   *

An empty pocket is the heaviest thing in the world.

* * *

The most important quality a writer must have is a smal appetite.

* * *

A rich man's daughter is always a beauty.

Making Merry Over Their Shortcomings

There are probably more stories concerning Jews than about any other people. Here are a few, exemplifying the wit of the Jews, but note from Freud is worth recording.

The Jewish jokes made up by non-Jews are nearly all brutal buffooneries in which the wit is spoiled by the fact that the Jew appears as a comic figure to a stranger. The Jewish jokes which originate with Jews admit this, but they know their merits as well as their real shortcomings.'

A Jew is alone in a railway compartment. A Negro enters, sits opposite him, takes out a Yiddish newspaper, and begins to read it. After a few minutes, the Jew, unable to contain himself any longer, taps the Negro on the knee to get his attention, and asks him incredulously:

Black isn't enough for you?

*   *   *

Three nuclear scientists, an American, a Frenchman, and a Jew, had become contaminated, and there was little hope of saving them.

Each was asked to express a last wish.

Said the American: I would like to meet the President and be decorated by him.

The Frenchman: I, too, would like to meet my President and receive the Legion of Honour.

And your request?, the Jew was asked.

A second opinion.

*　　　*　　　*

An orthodox rabbi awoke very early one Saturday morning. It was a beautiful morning, and being a golf fanatic, he decided to have a round before anybody was up, and he would still be in time for his synagogue service.

Alone on the course, he teed up and drove off. He did the first hole, which was par four, in three.

In heaven there was a turmoil. The angel Gabriel pleaded with the Almighty to punish the rabbi, but the Almighty just smiled.

The second hole was accomplished in two.

Again the angel Gabriel pleaded unsuccessfully for the rabbi to be punished for breaking the sabbath.

The rabbi did the third hole in one, and followed this by doing the fourth in one.

'Please, Almighty, punish this sinner,' pleaded Gabriel.

'Isn't he punished enough?' murmured the Almighty. 'He will never be able to tell this to anybody.'

*　　　*　　　*

A Russian officer and an old Russian rabbi shared a carriage on the trans-Siberian railway. For the first 150 miles there was silence. Then the officer seized the old rabbi by the lapels of his coat, and asked him, 'Why are you Jews so clever? Why do you rule the world?'

'Clever?' murmured the Jew. 'I suppose it's because we eat fish.'

Silence again for the next 100 miles. Then the old Jew opened a parcel, took out a salt-herring, and ate it all. The Russian officer watched him closely, and then asked how many herrings the rabbi had.

'Twelve.'

'I'll buy the lot,' said the officer. 'How much do you want?'

'Twenty roubles,' said the rabbi.

The deal was made, and after the officer had eaten his first herring, he suddenly seized the Jew again by his lapels, and said, 'I gave you twenty roubles for the herrings. In Moscow I can buy them for a few kopecks.'

'There, you see,' smiled the rabbi, 'it's beginning to work already.'

*　　　*　　　*

General de Gaulle was presented with a length of fine cloth. He sent for the best tailor in Paris, and demanded that a suit be made from the cloth. After measuring the cloth the tailor protested that there was not nearly enough cloth for so big a man as de Gaulle. The General took the cloth with him on his travels, and received a similar reply in Bonn, Rome and Moscow.

Finally, he landed in Israel, and sent for the best tailor in

I

Tel Aviv. The tailor measured the cloth, and asked the General if he would like an extra pair of trousers with the suit. De Gaulle was amazed.

'How is it,' he asked, 'that in the world's capitals nobody could make me a suit, and you can provide me even with an extra pair of trousers?'

'You see,' beamed the Jewish tailor, 'in those countries you are a very big man, but here you are just a small man.'

*   *   *

A Jew survived the gas chambers, having lost every one of his relatives.

The resettlement officer asked him where he would like to go.

'Australia,' he replied.

'But that's so far,' said the officer.

'From where?' asked the Jew.

*   *   *

An Israeli recruit reports for duty.

'Which branch do you want to join?' asks the sergeant.

'Air Force?'

'No,' replies the recruit.

'Navy?'

'No.'

'Infantry?'

'No.'

'What do you want to be then?'

'I want to be the unknown soldier.'

* * *

An immigrant in Israel takes his first walk. He comes to an orange grove, picks an orange, and settles himself in the shade of the tree to enjoy it.

The owner of the grove finds him there.

'What's the idea?' he asks. 'Haven't you heard of the eighth commandment?'

The immigrant smiles, and says, 'How beautiful is our holy land of Israel. One eats luscious fruit in the shade of a tree, and at the same time one enjoys a study of the Bible.'

* * *

A very poor and persecuted immigrant arrived in New York. Taking his first walk he was knocked unconscious by a Rolls-Royce car. After a short while he opened his eyes to find himself in the arms of a uniformed chauffeur, who was tending him with the greatest solicitude and care. Murmured the old Jew:

Am I already in heaven?

* * *

Max Liebermann, famous Berlin artist, annoyed by the chatter of a lady he was painting, finally shut her up by saying:

Another word from you, and I paint you as you are.

* * *

Hearing of a marvellous tailor in a little Polish town, a visitor ordered a pair of trousers. The garment was not delivered by the time the visitor left the town.

Six years elapsed and the visitor returned to the town. Promptly the tailor arrived with the trousers.

VISITOR: God made the Universe in six days, and you needed six years to make one pair of trousers.

TAILOR *(lovingly stroking the trousers)*: True, but look at the world, and look at the trousers!

* * *

'A terrible thing,' says Jacob to his friend. 'My daughter is to be married tomorrow and I promised a dowry of five thousand roubles. Now half the dowry is missing.'

'So what?' replies the friend. 'One usually pays only half of the promised dowry.'

'That's the half that's missing.'

* * *

An American Jew admired the Mann Auditorium in Israel.

'Named after the writer, Thomas Mann?' said the American to his guide.

'No.'

'Heinrich Mann, then?'

'No. It's named after Frederic Mann.'

'What did he write?'

'Cheques!'

* * *

'Why don't you take X for your assistant?'
'Because he was engaged to my wife and then broke it off.
I don't want an employee who is cleverer than I am.'

*   *   *

A Jew was drowning in the River Volga, and cried for
help. Two Russian policemen ran to the bank, saw that it
was a Jew and decided to let him drown.
As he was going down for the third time, he shouted as
loudly as he could: 'Down with the Tsar! To hell with the
Tsar!'
Hearing such seditious words, the policemen dived in,
pulled him out, and arrested him.

*   *   *

First Jew: My wife asks for money all day long.
Second Jew: What does she do with it?
First Jew: How should I know? I never give her any.

*   *   *

*Chaim Weizmann, first President of Israel, and President
Truman of USA were discussing their relative positions. Said
Weizmann:*

You are the President of a nation of 150 million people.
I am the President of a nation of a million Presidents.

*   *   *

A Jew explaining to his wife Einstein's Theory of Relativity:

If I have only a single hair on my head, that's too little. But if I have one single hair of yours in my soup, that's too much.

*   *   *

Two Jewish scholars meet. Says one: 'Tell me, do you live from the outside in, or from the inside out?' Replies the other:

If you put it that way, the answer is 'yes'.

*   *   *

Attributed to General Rabin, one of the architects of the Israeli victory in the 'Six Day War' of 1967. Asked why his men fought so well, he replied:

I told them that the war was a serious business, and that I wanted them to act like business men. They did. When I said 'Charge', they over-charged.

*   *   *

A Rothschild had died. Outside his house stood a poor Jew sobbing in heart-breaking fashion. A servant, taking pity on the man, came out to console him. 'Why do you weep so?' he asked. 'After all, you are not a relative.'
'That's why I'm crying,' came the swift reply.

*   *   *

Isaac was recruited for the Israeli artillery corps. Seemingly intelligent, he was awkward and clumsy, and had no interest in the service. His officer, kindly disposed towards him, drew him aside one day, and said:

Isaac, you are out of place among us. I advise you to buy a cannon and make yourself independent.

*   *   *

A 'schnorrer' (habitual beggar), who was a regular Sunday-dinner guest at a certain house, appeared one day accompanied by a young stranger, who prepared to seat himself at the table.

'Who is that?' demanded the host.

'He became my son-in-law last week,' replied the 'schnorrer', 'and I have agreed to supply his board for the first year.'

*   *   *

The storm was terrific and the ship seemed doomed. A venerable saint and a notorious sinner, two of the passengers, stood together.

'Save me, O Lord!' cried the sinner.

'Hush,' whispered the saint. 'Don't let God know you're here, or it will be the end of all of us.'

*   *   *

A poor man came to his rabbi for advice.

'Help me, Rabbi! I have a wife and nine children. I cannot support them. Every year my wife gives me a new child. What shall I do?'

'Do?' answered the rabbi. 'Take my advice and do nothing.'

*   *   *

A bridegroom of forty was chided because he had married a girl of twenty. He answered:

It's not as bad as it seems. When she looks at me she feels ten years older, and when I look at her I feel ten years younger. So, really, we're both thirty.

*   *   *

Three Jewish architects arrived simultaneously at the Gates of Heaven. The Angel Gabriel was there to welcome them, but warned them that there was only one vacant place in Paradise at the moment, and that he would award it to the one who had put up a worth-while building for the least money.

Said the first: I built a famous police headquarters for a few coppers.

Said the second: That's nothing. I put up the most renowned opera house for a song.

Said the third: It's mine. I built the United Nations for nothing.

*   *   *

A rich philanthropist, entering a Jewish restaurant, noticed a beggar, to whom he had given alms, with a large dish of smoked salmon. 'Aren't you ashamed of yourself?' he asked. 'This morning you came to beg from me, and now I find you in this expensive restaurant eating smoked salmon.' Answered the beggar:

What do you expect? When I haven't any money, *I can't* eat smoked salmon. When I have some money *I musn't* eat smoked salmon. When *am* I to eat smoked salmon?

*   *   *

Two Jews were looking at the magnificent tomb of a member of the Rothschild family. Said one of them:

Mmmm! The way some people live!

*   *   *

A Jew calls on the leader of the community for aid, explaining that his home and all that he possessed had been destroyed by fire. Have you any document from your rabbi proving all this? he was asked.

I had one, but that too was burnt.

*   *   *

When a Russian Jew tells a joke to a peasant, he laughs

three times – when you tell it, when you explain it, and when he finally understands it.

A landowner laughs twice – when the Jew tells it and when he explains it, because he never understands it.

An army officer laughs only once – when the Jew tells the joke, because he never lets him get any further.

But when he begins to tell the joke to another Jew, he immediately interrupts him to tell him it is an old one, and demonstrates how much better he can tell it himself.

*   *   *

The old man was dying, surrounded by his weeping family.

'Are you there, Sarah?' he asked his wife in a feeble voice.

'Yes,' came the reply.

'And Jacob?'

'Yes.'

'And Joseph?'

'Yes.'

'And Benjamin?'

'Yes.'

'And Rachel?'

'Yes.'

'And Rosie?'

'Yes.'

'Well,' he cried, sitting bolt upright. 'And who's looking after the shop?'

*   *   *

A Jew who had been unsuccessful in business offered this prayer:

O Lord, help me in my business! You help complete strangers, so why not help me?

    *   *   *

A lady trying to impress the American rabbi, Stephen Wise, boasted that one of her ancestors witnessed the signing of the Declaration of Independence. The rabbi replied:

Mine were present at the giving of the Ten Commandments.

    *   *   *

Two stories attributed to George Jessel:

A girl heavy with child – and out of wedlock – went from doctor to doctor, to have it removed, but without success. One day she heard of a well-known politician, and went to see him. 'They tell me you will help the humblest,' she said, and told him of her predicament.

'I'll be happy to find you a good husband,' the man replied.

'Oh, no!' said the girl, 'I don't want to bear this child.'

'Then there is nothing I can do,' said the kindly old statesman.

'There is,' said the girl. 'Just put your hand on my tummy for a minute.'

The puzzled politician asked, 'Why should I do that?'

'Because,' replied the girl, 'people say that what you put your hand to, nothing comes of it.'

*   *   *

A Catholic girl and a Jewish boy fell madly in love. But their religious beliefs intervened. The Irish Catholic mother advised her daughter to 'sell him a bill of goods. Teach him the beauty and joys of Catholicism – make him be a Catholic.'

The girl did. She sold him and sold him, and the wedding date was set. One day before the marriage the girl came home and sobbed. 'The marriage is off.'

'Why,' said the mother, 'didn't you sell him?'

And the girl answered: 'I sold him. . . . Now he wants to be a priest.'

They Even Laughed at Hitler

Even in the darkest days of their chequered history, the Jews managed to laugh at their persecutors.

The Aryan test

The rueful Jewish question was: Are you an Aryan or are you learning English?

* * *

The Host

A blasphemous rhyme which went the rounds:

Our Leader, who art our host,
Give us each day the bread you boast;
Not just cabbage, turnips and herring,
Give us what you eat, and what you give Goering.

* * *

A little girl in Germany told her school-teacher that her cat had given birth to five kittens, so very beautiful kittens, and 'they are all darling little Nazis', added the girl. A month later an official of the German propaganda ministry visited the school, and the teacher asked the little girl to repeat her story.

'Yes, Herr Inspector,' she said. 'My cat gave birth to five beautiful kittens, and they are all darling little Social-Democrats.'

'What,' shouted the teacher, 'I thought you told me they were darling little Nazis.'

'Oh, yes, they were,' replied the little girl, 'but that was four weeks ago. Their eyes are now open, you see.'

*   *   *

Cure for homesickness

The purser of a British liner had to visit the cabin of a Jewish refugee. On the table was a photograph of Hitler.

'Gosh,' said the purser, 'what are you, a refugee, doing with the Fuehrer's portrait?'

'Ah,' said the refugee, 'it's a wrench to leave one's home. I keep the picture as an antidote to homesickness.'

*   *   *

What is the difference between Prime Minister Neville Chamberlain and Reichsführer Adolf Hitler?

Chamberlain takes his weekends in the country and Hitler takes his countries in the weekends.

*   *   *

THEY EVEN LAUGHED AT HITLER

A Gestapo agent questioned a small boy.

'Have you a picture of Hitler hanging in your house?'

'No.'

'Have you one of Goering and Goebbels hanging in your house?'

'No,' replied the boy, 'but when my father gets out of concentration camp he said he's going to hang them all.'

*   *   *

A Jew arrives at his scanty breakfast table in a supremely happy mood.

'Why so happy?' asks his sad wife. 'You've nothing to laugh about.'

'Oh,' replied her husband, 'I had a wonderful dream. I went to Hitler's funeral. It was marvellous. The coffin went up and down thirty-six times, so great was the applause.'

*   *   *

A German mother taught her little girl to end her prayers with 'Thank God for Adolf Hitler'.

'What do I say if Hitler dies?' asked the child.

'Oh, then you just say "Thank God".'

*   *   *

A Jew is being grilled by a Nazi officer for feeding his solitary chicken. Finally the Jew says:

I don't feed him any more. I give him a few coppers an
he buys his own food.

* * *

Two frightened Jews met in Vienna.
'How are you?' asked one.
'So-so,' replied the other.
'And how's your brother?'
'Oh, he's wonderful. He's the Chief Rabbi of Berlin.'
'My, my,' exclaimed the other admiringly, 'and that as
Jew!'

* * *

Letter of a Jewish woman to a friend:

My dear Lisl,

Since Hitler took over Czechoslovakia, life is wonderfu
We are all very happy and everything is fine.

Love from Maria.

PS
Uncle Rudla, who did not agree, was buried yesterday

* * *

A French Jew's diplomatic witty crack about Goerin
'Le chevalier sans beurre et sans brioches.'

* * *

Hitler made one of his famous speeches. In the front row sat a little Jew who during the whole speech shook his head and smiled. *(This was before Hitler became Chancellor.)* After the speech Hitler had the little Jew brought to him, and asked him why he had behaved as he did.

'I was only amazed,' replied the Jew, 'and asked myself some questions.'

'About what?' snorted Hitler.

Said the Jew: 'To remember Pharaoh and the exit from Egypt we celebrate Passover and eat Matzos. To remember Haman we celebrate Purim and eat three-cornered poppyseed cakes. I wonder what holiday we will celebrate, and what we will eat after your exit.'

*　　　*　　　*

Some Nazis surrounded an old Jew and asked him who was responsible for the war.

'The Jews,' answered the old man, and then added, 'and the cyclists.'

'Why the cyclists?' asked the puzzled Nazis.

'Why the Jews?' answered the old man.

*　　　*　　　*

Two Jews in Berlin discussing their sad plight.

'Terrible,' said one. 'Persecutions, no rations, discrimination, quotas, and Hitler on top of it. Sometimes I think we would have been better off if we had never been born!'

'Sure,' answered the other, 'but who can be so lucky? No one in twenty thousand.'

*　　　*　　　*

Two Jews meet in Cologne.
'Can you lend me a cigarette paper?' asks one.
'Sorry,' replies the other, 'I used my last one to wrap up my meat ration.'

pigrams

*is form of writing was much in favour with Jewish scholars
poets, because of the play of wit which is permitted.*

ac ben Jacob (1801-1863)
huanian poet

scribbler

> Zimron, poet, makes his will,
> Orders with his latest breath,
> That the offspring of his quill
> Shall be published after death.
> A gloomy prospect 'tis for all, we say
> We hope he'll live for ever and a day.

another writer

'is cruel that critics should love to belabour
)ur plagiarist poet with stock and with stone,
or, if he has borrowed the thoughts of his neighbour,
'is harsh to assume that the faults are his own.

The departed doctor

> Our doctor is dead; ah well, dry your tears;
> Death's sad, but what use to resent it?
> For, if he had lived another few years,
> There'd be none of us here to lament it.

The miser

> I'm growing old, and hence ere long shall fare;
> How I should love to be my only heir.

The devoted lover

> Who kneels before his lady fair,
> And begs her love in humble mode,
> Is like the camel on his knees,
> Eager to bear his master's load.

Wise people

> Think not that those are purely sages
> Whose beard and pouch are large of size,
> Or else the goats through all the ages
> Must, too, be classed among the wise.

Doctor Pill

> Once, when I was very ill,
> I called in famous Doctor Pill;

He cured me, true; I saw his bill –
And find myself a sick man still.

*   *   *

mmanuel of Rome (1265-1330)
Iebrew poet

Make every man your friend
However poor or weak,
With every solace tend
The humble and the meek.
Do you ask the reason why?
The giant feels the stinging fly.

*   *   *

hem-Tob Falaquera (1225-1290)
panish philosopher and poet

Adapt yourself to time and circumstance,
So will you be untroubled every day;
If you meet a lion roar,
But if you meet an ass, just bray.

My friend, speak always once, but listen twice,
This, I would have you know, is sound advice;
For God hath given you and all your peers
A single mouth, friend, but a pair of ears.

*   *   *

145

M Mandelkern (1846-1902)
Russian poet and author

The reason why

> The doctors talk Latin, 'tis said,
> When they meet in the sickroom. Oh, why?
> They think that a language that's dead
> Suits the man who is going to die.

> How passing strange it is of late,
> The deaths have numbered almost nil;
> 'Tis not so startling when I state,
> That Doctor Fell himself is ill.

A husband's complaint

> By heaven's favour, I possess
> Two treasures dearer far than gold;
> A wife and cellar; I confess
> The wine is young, the woman's old.
> And naught could now my joy enhance
> The crowd of mortal men among,
> Unless it happened that, perchance,
> The wine were old, the woman young.

*   *   *

Abraham Ibn Hasdai (circa 1230)
Spanish scholar

> Go not too frequently thy friend to see,
> Lest they grow weary of the sight of thee;
> When rain is scanty then we pray for more,
> But love not one continuous downpour.

*   *   *

Yehudah Halevi (circa 1085-1140)
Spanish poet and philosopher

The first grey hair

> One day I saw a grey hair in my head;
> I plucked it out, when to me it said,
> 'Think, if thou wilt, that thou art rid of me,
> I've twenty friends who soon will mock at thee.'

*   *   *

Judah Jeiteles (1773-1838)
Austrian scholar

Epitaph for a judge

> Here lies Judge X—, he's done with legal tort,
> And sleeps as soundly as he did in court.

To a scribbler

> Your book, how tragically you said it,
> Hath made your patient vigils keep;
> Be comforted, for when I read it,
> It lulled me peacefully to sleep.

*   *   *

Juda Ben Zeev (1764-1811)
Polish grammarian

> A miser once dreamed he had given away
> Some bread to a beggar he had met in the day.
> In terror he woke and he solemnly swore,
> That the rest of his life he would slumber no more.

*   *   *

Abraham Ibn Ezra (1092-1167)
Hebrew-Spanish poet

The courage that laughs at misfortunes

> In vain I labour, all my toil is vain,
> For never can I boast of riches' gain.
> The Fates have frowned upon me since my birth,
> And failure is my portion here on earth.
> Were I to take the notion in my head
> To deal in shrouds, the cerements of the dead;

Then to establish how ill-starred am I,
No man who lives on earth would ever die;
Or should I try to make wax candles pay,
The sun would shine by night as well as day.

*   *   *

M Schlesinger (d 1829)

The gourmand

> My piteous plight oft makes me weep –
> I cannot eat while I am asleep.

*   *   *

An epitaph

> Here lies Nachson, a man of great renown,
> Who won much glory in his native town;
> 'Twas hunger killed him, and they let him die,
> They give him statues now, and gaze, and sigh,
> While Nachson lived, he badly wanted bread,
> Now he is gone, he gets a stone instead.

*   *   *

From the Jewish Theological Seminary of America

A human life is like a single letter in the alphabet. It can
be meaningless, or it can be part of a great meaning.

Acknowledgments

We have spared no effort to trace the ownership of all copyright material, and we express our regret if we have innocently erred.

We are grateful to the many authors and publishers, who have allowed us to quote from their works, and for the great interest they have shown in our labours.

Acknowledgments are due to the following:

Vicki Baum, *I Know What I'm Worth* – Michael Joseph; David Higham Associates.

S N Behrman, *Lord Duveen* – Random House.

Art Buchwald, *Don't Forget to Write* – Victor Gollancz; *Art Buchwald's Paris* – Chatto and Windus.

Eddie Cantor, *The Way I See It* – © 1959 by Eddie Cantor; Prentice-Hall Inc.

Joseph Chotzner, *Hebrew Satire* – Kegan Paul.

Art Cohn, *Nine Lives of Mike Todd* – Hutchinson. © Mrs Art Cohn.

Sammy Davis Jr, *Yes, I Can* – Cassell & Co; Farrar, Straus & Giroux, Inc.

Brian Epstein, *A Cellarful of Noise* – Souvenir Press.

Jacob Epstein, *Autobiography* – Hulton Press.

David Ewen, *The Story of Jerome Kern* – Henry Holt.

Montagu Glass, *Lucky Numbers* – Doubleday & Co, Inc.;

William Heinemann. *Potash and Perlmutter* – Samuel French Inc., New York.

Louis Golding, *The World I Knew* – Hutchinson.

Philip Guedella, *Masters of Men; Supers and Superman* – Constable. © Nellie Guedella.

Samuel Hoffenstein, *Pencil in the Air* – Doubleday & Co, Inc. © David Hoffenstein.

George Jessell, *Jessel Anyone?* – Prentice Hall Inc. *Make a Speech* – Grayson Publishing Corpn.

Otto Kahn, *Of Many Things* – Jonathan Cape.

Arthur Kober, *Parm Me* – Constable.

Axel Madsen, *Billy Wilder* – Secker & Warburg.

Groucho Marx, *The Groucho Letters* – Michael Joseph. *Life with Groucho* – Simon & Schuster, Inc.

André Maurois, *The Art of Living* – The Bodley Head. © Mme M Maurois.

George Jean Nathan, *Testament of a Critic* – Alfred Knopf Inc.

S J Perelman, *The Most of S J Perelman* – Simon & Schuster Inc.; William Heinemann.

Billy Rose, *Wine, Women and Words* – Simon & Schuster Inc.

Herbert Viscount Samuel, OM, *A Book of Quotations* – Cresset Press.

Haim Schwarzbaum, *Jewish and World Folk Lore* – Walter de Gruyter and Co.

Chaim Weizmann, *Trial and Error* – Hamish Hamilton; Harper & Row, Inc.; © 1949 by the Weizmann Foundation.

Vera Weizmann and David Tutaev, *The Impossible Takes Longer* – Hamish Hamilton; Harper and Row Inc.

ACKNOWLEDGMENTS

Humbert Wolfe, *ABC of the Theatre* – Cresset Press.
Israel Zangwill, *Children of the Ghetto* – William Heinemann; Macmillan & Co, New York.

We are especially indebted to the British Museum, and to
the *Daily Express*, its former Chief Librarian, E W Merrett
and to the present Chief, Edward Brisland.